POCKET
LONDON

TOP EXPERIENCES · LOCAL LIFE

Thr Westminster 44, M54

Natural History Museum 150 M155

Transport National Gallery 66, M71
Museum Covent Gardens, M71
Tower of London St. Pauls Cathedral 108, M116

Thr London Eye 135, M132 book online

Thr Churchill war room 56, M54

Thr St. James Park M54 (MAP)

**STEVE FALLON, DAMIAN HARPER,
LAUREN KEITH, MASOVAIDA MORGAN,
TASMIN WABY**

Contents

Plan Your Trip 4

St Paul's Cathedral (p108)
TOLGA_TEZCAN/GETTY IMAGES ©

COVID-19

We have re-checked every business in this book before publication to ensure that it is still open after the COVID-19 outbreak. However, the economic and social impacts of COVID-19 will continue to be felt long after the outbreak has been contained, and many businesses, services and events referenced in this guide may experience ongoing restrictions. Some businesses may be temporarily closed, have changed their opening hours and services, or require bookings; some unfortunately could have closed permanently. We suggest you check with venues before visiting for the latest information.

London's Top Experiences

Wander through time at the British Museum (p88)

KIEV.VICTOR/SHUTTERSTOCK © GREAT COURT ARCHITECT: NORMAN FOSTER

Tickets and Membership

Stand in awe at St Paul's Cathedral (p108)

VICTOR MOUSSA/SHUTTERSTOCK ©

Get with the trends at Tate Modern (p128)

CLAUDIO DIVIZIA/SHUTTERSTOCK ©

Explore nature at the Natural History Museum (p150)

I WEI HUANG/SHUTTERSTOCK ©

See the Crown Jewels at the Tower of London (p112)

LIOX/SHUTTERSTOCK ©

DAN BRECKWOLDT/SHUTTERSTOCK ©

Walk the stately Houses of Parliament (p50)

Visit kings and queens at Westminster Abbey (p44)

Catch amazing art at the National Gallery (p66)

Stroll among the artworks at Victoria & Albert Museum (p146)

CHRISPICTURES/SHUTTERSTOCK ©

MYRIAM KEOGH/SHUTTERSTOCK ©

Wave to royalty at Buckingham Palace (p48)

Tour regal Hampton Court Palace (p198)

TOM GREEN/GETTY IMAGES ©

PAJOR PAWEL/SHUTTERSTOCK ©

Ponder the stars at the Royal Observatory and Greenwich Park (p192)

Dining Out

London's hospitality scene is now up there with the best dining destinations, but it pays to do your research; there is a lot of mediocre here, too. London's strongest asset is its incredible diversity: from street-food markets to high-end dining with epic views – and global cuisines from Afghan to Zambian – it's an A to Z of foodie experiences.

World Food

One of the joys of eating out in London is the sheer choice. For historical reasons Indian cuisine is widely available, and Asian cuisines in general are popular. You'll find dozens of Chinese, Vietnamese, Thai, Japanese and Korean restaurants, as well as elaborate fusion establishments blending flavours from different parts of Asia.

Middle Eastern cuisine is also well covered. Continental Europe cuisines – French, Italian, Greek, Spanish, Scandinavian etc – are easy to find, with many excellent modern European establishments. Restaurants serving ethnic cuisines tend to congregate where their home community is based.

British Food

Modern British food has become a cuisine in its own right, championing traditional ingredients such as root vegetables, smoked fish, shellfish, game, salt-marsh lamb, sausages, offal, black pudding, bone marrow and secondary cuts of meat.

Gastropubs

Not long ago, the pub was where you went for a drink, with maybe a packet of potato crisps to soak up the alcohol. The birth of the gastropub in the 1990s, however, means that today just about every establishment serves full meals. The quality varies widely, from microwaved dishes to vegan choices and five-star cuisine with impressive wine lists.

BHARAT RAWAIL/SHUTTERSTOCK ©

Best British

St John The restaurant that inspired the revival of British cuisine. (p188)

Dinner by Heston Blumenthal Winning celebration of British cuisine. (p161)

Launceston Place Magnificent food, presentation and service. (p162)

Hook Camden Town What sort of British list would it be without fish and chips? (p176)

Best European

Padella Cheap and flavourful homemade pasta in Borough Market. (pictured; p137)

Skylon Stunning Thames vistas; fine international menu. (p138)

Delaunay Grand mittel-European ambience. (p78)

Chiltern Firehouse Luxe, celebrity-attracting, good-looking spot. (p98)

Best Indian & Asian

Gymkhana Splendid club-style Raj environment and top cuisine. (p58)

Smoking Goat Exceptional Thai in mod-industrial surrounds. (p188)

A Wong Deftly embracing flavours from all four corners of China. (p162)

Miyama Gem of a Japanese restaurant with oodles of choice. (p121)

Kanada-Ya Join the queue for its superb *tonkotsu* ramen. (p78)

Bookings & Discounts

○ Many top-end restaurants offer great-value set lunch menus. À la carte lunch prices can be cheaper than for dinner.

○ Internet booking service Open Table (www.opentable.co.uk) offers discounts at selected restaurants.

London on a Plate
Pie & Mash

The pie: minced beef for purists, but variations allowed

Liquor: a parsley and vinegar sauce; if you don't like the sound of liquor, there's always gravy

Creamy mashed potato, smothered in sauce

★ Top Spots for Pie & Mash

Battersea Pie Station (☏020-7240 9566; www.batterseapie.co.uk; lower ground fl, 28 The Market, Covent Garden, WC2; mains £7-10; ⊙11am-7.30pm Mon-Fri, 10am-8pm Sat, 11am-7pm Sun; Ⓤ Covent Garden)

Goddards at Greenwich (☏020-8305 9612; www.goddardsatgreenwich.co.uk; 22 King William Walk, SE10; pie & mash £4.40-8.50; ⊙10am-7.30pm Sun-Thu, to 8pm Fri & Sat; Ⓤ Cutty Sark)

Cockney's Pie and Mash (☏020-8960 9409; www.facebook.com/cockneyspiemashW10; 314 Portobello Rd, W10; pie & mash £3.50; ⊙11.30am-5pm Tue-Sat; Ⓤ Ladbroke Grove, Westbourne Park)

Pie & Mash in London

From the middle of the 19th century until just after WWII, the staple lunch for many Londoners was a spiced-eel pie (eels were once plentiful in the Thames) served with mashed potatoes and liquor. The staple modern-day filling is minced beef (curried meat is also good). Pie-and-mash restaurants are rarely fancy, but they offer something of a time-travel culinary experience.

Goddards at Greenwich

PHOTO: OPTICAL/SHUTTERSTOCK ©

CHRIS LAWRENCE TRAVEL/SHUTTERSTOCK ©

Bar Open

You need only glance at William Hogarth's Gin Lane prints from 1751 to realise that Londoners and alcohol have a colourful history. The metropolis offers a huge variety of venues to wet your whistle in – from cosy neighbourhood pubs to glitzy all-night clubs and five-star hotel cocktail bars, and all points in between.

Pubs

At the heart of London social life, the pub is one of the capital's great social levellers. Order almost anything you like, but beer is the staple. Some pubs specialise, offering drinks from local microbreweries, fruit beers, organic ciders and other rarer beverages. Others, especially gastropubs, proffer strong wine lists. Some pubs have delightful beer gardens – crucial in summer. Others are exquisitely historic. Most pubs and bars open at 11am, closing at 11pm from Monday to Saturday and 10.30pm on Sunday. Some pubs stay open longer, often until midnight, sometimes until 1am or 2am.

Bars & Clubs

Bars are generally open later than pubs but close earlier than clubs. They may have DJs and a small dance floor, door charges after 11pm, more modern decor, and fancier (and pricier) drinks, including cocktails, than pubs. If you're up for clubbing, London has an embarrassment of riches: choose between legendary establishments such as Fabric or smaller clubs with up-and-coming DJs. Dress to impress (no jeans or trainers) in posh clubs, and check the dress code. Further east, things are laid-back and chill. Cocktail bars are undergoing a renaissance, so you'll find lots of upmarket options serving increasingly inventive concoctions.

Best Pubs

Lock Tavern Camden pub with roof terrace and live music. (p177)

PHAUSTOV/SHUTTERSTOCK ©

Lamb Wreathed in yester-year loveliness. (p102)

Windsor Castle High up on Campden Hill Rd, with a fabulous beer garden. (p164)

Best Historic Pubs

George Inn History, age-old charm and National Trust designation. (p141)

Lamb & Flag Atmospheric and creaky old-timer. (p80)

Princess Louise Oozing Victorian charm and period panache. (p102)

Best Bars

Dukes London Classic bar at the heart of London; best Martinis in town. (p60)

American Bar Stylish art deco gem. (p80)

Searcys at the Gherkin Cocktails with 360-degree city views. (p123)

Seabird South Bank rooftop outpost with ace views. (p140)

Gordon's Wine Bar Ancient, underground, candle-lit nook off the Strand. (p81)

Best Clubs

Fabric London's most famous superclub. (p190)

Heaven The gay club in London. (p81)

Worth a Trip

The riverside location and fine food make the bay-windowed **White Cross** (pictured; ☎020-8940 6844; www.thewhitecrossrichmond.com; Water Lane, TW9; ⏰11am-11pm Mon-Fri, 10am-10.30pm Sat & Sun; 🛜; Ⓤ Richmond) from 1748 on the site of a former friary a winner. There are entrances for low and high tides, and wellies are provided if wading is necessary.

London in a Glass
Pimm's & Lemonade

Sunshine, shades and good company to serve

One part Pimm's, three parts lemonade

Highball glass (not a pint, this is a classy drink) and ice

For additional flourish, lemon, lime and cucumber slices

Strawberries, orange and fresh mint – the bare minimum

★ Top Three Places for Pimm's

Garden Gate (p177)

Spaniard's Inn (p181)

Windsor Castle (p164)

Pimm's & Lemonade in London

Pimm's, a gin-based fruity spirit, is the quintessential British summer drink: no sunny afternoon in a beer garden would be complete without a glass (or jug) of it. It is served with lemonade, mint and fresh fruit. Most pubs and bars serve it, although they may only have all the trimmings in summer.

Windsor Castle (p164)

ALENA VEASEY/SHUTTERSTOCK ©

Treasure Hunt

From charity-shop finds to designer bags, there are thousands of ways to spend your hard-earned cash in London. Many of the big-name shopping attractions, such as Harrods, Hamleys, Camden Market and Old Spitalfields Market, have become must-sees in their own right. With so many temptations, you'll give your wallet a workout.

WILLY BARTON/SHUTTERSTOCK ©

Chain Stores

Many bemoan the fact that chains have taken over the main shopping centres, leaving independent shops struggling to balance the books. But since they're cheap, fashionable and always conveniently located, Londoners (and others) keep going back for more. As well as familiar overseas retailers, such as Gap, H&M, Urban Outfitters and Zara, you'll find plenty of home-grown chains, including luxury womenswear brand Karen Millen (www.karenmillen.com) and global giant Topshop (www.topshop.com).

Opening Hours

London shops generally open from 9am or 10am to 6pm or 7pm, Monday to Saturday. The majority of West End (Oxford St, Soho and Covent Garden), Chelsea, Knightsbridge, Kensington, Greenwich and Hampstead shops also open on Sunday, typically from noon to 6pm, but sometimes 10am to 4pm. Shops in the West End open late (to 9pm) on Thursday; those in Chelsea, Knightsbridge and Kensington open late on Wednesday. If a major market is in swing on a certain day, neighbouring shops will probably also fling open their doors.

Best Department Stores

Harrods Garish, stylish and just the right side of kitsch, yet perennially popular. (p165)

Liberty Irresistible blend of contemporary styles in old-fashioned atmosphere. (p83)

CHRISPICTURES/SHUTTERSTOCK ©

Fortnum & Mason London's oldest grocery store, with staff still dressed in tails. (pictured above right; p61)

Best Shopping Areas

West End Grand confluence of big names for the well heeled and well dressed.

Knightsbridge Harrods and other top names servicing London's wealthiest residents.

Best Bookshops

John Sandoe Books Fine, knowledgeable customer service and terrific stock. (p165)

Hatchards London's oldest bookshop (1797), with fantastic stock and plenty of events. (p61)

Lutyens & Rubinstein Choice selection; run by a literary agency. (p167)

Foyles Once a byword for confusion, now a joy to browse for bibliophiles. (p82)

Libreria Celebrate the printed page in this cultural treasure trove. (p190)

Best for Gifts

Penhaligon's Beautiful range of perfumes and home fragrances, all made in England. (p61)

Aida Indie brands, unique pieces, and a cafe to boot. (p190)

Suck UK Fun, creative and quirky gifts you won't want to give away. (p143)

Tax-Exempt Purchases

In stores displaying a 'tax free' sign, visitors from non-EU countries are entitled to recoup the 20% VAT on purchases. See www.gov.uk/tax-on-shopping/taxfree-shopping.

Top London Souvenirs

London Toys

Double-decker buses, Paddington bears, guards in bearskin hats: Hamleys (p84) is the place to go for iconic toys.

Music

London is brilliant for buying records. Try any of the umpteen vintage vinyl shops in Notting Hill, or head to Sounds of the Universe (p85) for rare pressings.

Tea

The British drink par excellence, with plenty of iconic names to choose from. For lovely packaging too, try Fortnum & Mason (pictured; p61) or Harrods (p165).

Vintage Fashion

Your London vintage clothing and footwear finds will forever be associated with your trip to the city. Start your search at Old Spitalfields Market (pictured; p191) or the Sunday UpMarket (p185) in the East End.

Collectable Books

London is heaven for bibliophiles, with numerous history-filled book-shops, brimming with covetable first editions and hard-to-find signed tomes. Try Hatchards (pictured; p61) or John Sandoe Books (p165).

Show Time

Whatever it is that sets your spirits soaring or your booty shaking, you'll find it in London. The city's been a world leader in theatre ever since a young man from Stratford-upon-Avon set up shop here in the 16th century. And if London started swinging in the 1960s, its live rock and pop scene has barely let up since.

Theatre

A night out at the theatre is as much a must-do London experience as a trip on the top deck of a double-decker bus. London's Theatreland in the dazzling West End – from Aldwych in the east, past Shaftesbury Ave to Regent St in the west – has a concentration of theatres only rivalled by New York's Broadway.

Classical Music

With multiple world-class orchestras and ensembles, quality venues, reasonable ticket prices, and performances covering the whole musical gamut from traditional crowd-pleasers to innovative compositions, London will satisfy even the fussiest classical-music buffs.

London Sounds

London has long been a generator of edgy and creative sounds. There's live music – rock, blues, jazz, folk, whatever – going on every night of the week in pulsing clubs, crowded pubs or roof-raising concert arenas.

Best Theatre

Shakespeare's Globe For the authentic open-air Elizabethan effect. (pictured; p141)

National Theatre Cutting-edge productions in a choice of three theatres. (p142)

Donmar Warehouse Intimate space with a diverse, pioneering edge. (p82)

Best for Classical Music & Opera

Royal Albert Hall Splendid and imposing red-brick Victorian concert hall south of Kensington Gardens. (p164)

Royal Opera House Venue of choice for classical ballet and opera buffs. (p82)

COWARDLION/SHUTTERSTOCK ©

Best Live Jazz

Ronnie Scott's Legendary Frith St jazz club in the West End. (p82)

606 Club Longstanding Chelsea basement with a loyal following. (p165)

Best Live Rock & Pop

Royal Albert Hall Gorgeous, grand and spacious, yet strangely intimate. (p164)

Jazz Cafe Despite the name, serves up sounds from all modern genres. (p178)

Best Dance

Royal Opera House World-class ballet. (p82)

Southbank Centre From Bollywood to break-dancing. (p135)

The Place Birthplace of modern English dance. (p104)

Best Music in Churches

Westminster Abbey Even-song and the city's finest organ concerts. (p44)

St Paul's Evensong at its most evocative. (p108)

St Martin-in-the-Fields Excellent classical-music concerts, many by candle-light. (p77)

Discount Tickets

Cut-price standby tickets are generally available at the National Theatre, the Barbican, the Royal Court Theatre and the Royal Opera House. Pick up in person on the day. Cheap £5 standing tickets are available daily at Shakespeare's Globe. Most mainstream and art-house cinemas offer discounts all day Monday (or Tuesday).

Museums & Galleries

London's museums and galleries head the list of the city's top attractions and not just for the rainy days that frequently send locals scurrying for shelter. Some of London's museums and galleries display incomparable collections that make them acknowledged leaders in their field.

GRAN TURISMO/SHUTTERSTOCK ©

Admission & Access

National museum collections (eg British Museum, National Gallery, Victoria & Albert Museum) are free, except for temporary exhibitions. Private galleries are usually free (or have a small admission fee), while smaller museums will charge an entrance fee, typically around £5 (book online for discounted tickets at some museums). National collections are generally open 10am to around 6pm, with one late night a week.

Specialist Museums

Whether you've a penchant for fans, London transport, ancient surgical techniques or commercial brands, you'll discover museums throughout the city with their own niche collections. Even for non-specialists, these museums can be fascinating to browse.

At Night

Evenings are a great time to visit, as there are fewer visitors. Many museums open late once a week, and several organise special nocturnal events to extend their range of activities and present the collection in a different mood. Check out museum websites for events, including sleepover opportunities, for both kids and kiddults.

Best Collections (All Free)

British Museum Supreme collection of rare artefacts and priceless heritage. (p88)

Victoria & Albert Museum Array of decorative arts and design in an awe-inspiring setting. (pictured above right; p146)

COWARDLION/SHUTTERSTOCK ©

National Gallery Tremendous gathering of largely pre-modern masters. (p66)

Tate Modern A feast of modern and contemporary art, wonderfully housed. (p128)

Natural History Museum Hit with kids and adults alike in one of London's most fabulous buildings. (pictured above left; p150)

Best House Museums

Sir John Soane's Museum Brimming with 18th-century curiosities. (p74)

Dennis Severs' House Home of a Huguenot silk weaver's family, preserved as if still inhabited. (p187)

Best Museum Architecture

Victoria & Albert Museum A building as beautiful as its diverse collection. (pictured above right; p146)

Natural History Museum Architectural lines straight from a Gothic fairy tale. (p150)

Best Small Museums

Old Operating Theatre Museum & Herb Garret Eye-opening foray into old-fashioned surgery techniques. (p136)

Museum of Brands Riveting collection of brand names through the ages. (p167)

Worth a Trip

The superb **Horniman Museum** (📞020-8699 1872; www.horniman.ac.uk; 100 London Rd, SE23; admission free; 🕙10am-5.30pm; 🚻; 🚆Forest Hill) comprises the collection of wealthy tea-merchant Frederick John Horniman, ranging from a dusty walrus and voodoo altars to a superb aquarium and a world-class music gallery.

Architecture

Waist-deep in history, London's rich seams of eye-opening antiquity appear at every turn. The city's architecture pens a beguiling biography, and a multitude of buildings are instantly recognisable landmarks. There's enough innovation to put a crackle in the air, but it never drowns out London's seasoned and centuries-old narrative.

London Style

Unlike some cities, London has never been methodically planned. Instead, it has developed in a haphazard fashion. As a result, London retains architectural reminders from every period of its long history, but they are often hidden: part of a Roman wall enclosed in the lobby of a modern building near St Paul's Cathedral, say, or a galleried coaching inn from the Restoration in a courtyard off Borough High St.

Best Modern Icons

Cheese Grater The 225m-tall Leadenhall Building in the form of a stepped wedge faces architect Richard Rogers' other icon, the Lloyd's of London building.

The Gherkin The 180m-tall bullet-shaped tower that seems to pop up at every turn; aka 30 St Mary Axe.

The Shard Needle-like 87-storey tower by Italian architect Renzo Piano. (p136)

Walkie Talkie This 37-storey, 160m-tall tower bulges in and bulges out, topped with the vast Sky Garden. (p118)

The Scalpel Razor sharp, pointy and angular addition to the ever-shifting City skyline.

Best Stately Architecture

Buckingham Palace The Queen's central London residence. (p48)

Houses of Parliament Extraordinary Victorian monument and seat of British parliamentary democracy. (p50)

Queen's House Beautiful Inigo Jones Palladian creation in charming Greenwich. (p197)

Hampton Court Palace Get lost in the famous maze or ghost hunt along Tudor hallways. (p198)

Painted Hall Admire this banqueting hall at the Old Royal Naval College. (p197)

MICHELE PRISCO/500PX ©

Best Early Architecture

Westminster Abbey Titanic milestone in London's ecclesiastical architectural history. (p44)

Houses of Parliament Westminster Hall has one of the finest hammerbeam roofs in the world. (p50)

Tower of London Legend, myth and bloodstained history converge in London's supreme bastion. (p112)

Hampton Court Palace The nation's most impressive and outstanding Tudor edifice, with a centuries-old maze to boot. (p198)

Best Monuments

Monument to the Great Fire of London Spiral your way up to panoramic views. (p119)

Albert Memorial Convoluted chunk of Victoriana. (p158)

Wellington Arch Topped by Europe's largest bronze sculpture. (p161)

Open House Architectural Tours

For one weekend at the end of September, hundreds of buildings normally closed to the public throw open their doors for **Open House London** (☎020-7383 2131; https://openhouselondon.open-city. org.uk; ☉Sep). Public buildings aren't forgotten either, with plenty of talks and tours. This architectural charity also sponsors talks with architectural tours to various areas of London held by sister organisation **Open City** (☎020-3006 7008; https://open-city.org.uk; 2½-3hr tours from £25.50).

For Kids

SIMA LEITNER/SHUTTERSTOCK ©

London is a fantastic place for children. The city's museums will fascinate all ages, and you'll find theatre, dance and music performances ideal for older kids. Playgrounds and parks, city farms and nature reserves are perfect for either toddler energy-busting or relaxation.

Museum Activities

London's museums are very child friendly, with dedicated children or family trails in virtually every one. Additionally, you'll find plenty of activities such as storytelling at the National Gallery, thematic backpacks to explore the British Museum, pop-up performances at the Victoria & Albert Museum, family audio guides at the Tate Modern, and art and crafts workshops at Somerset House, where kids can dance through the fountains in the courtyard in summer. The Science Museum has a marvellous interactive area downstairs called the Garden, where tots can splash around with water.

Eating with Kids

Many London cafes and restaurants are child-friendly and offer baby-changing facilities and high chairs. Pick your places with some awareness – avoid high-end and quieter restaurants if you have toddlers or babies. Note that gastropubs tend to be very family-friendly, but that drinking-only pubs may not allow children under the age of 16. If a children's menu isn't available, just ask for a smaller portion, which most restaurants will be happy to provide.

Best Sights, Activities & Shops

ZSL London Zoo Close to 750 species of animals and excellent Penguin Beach. (pictured above left; p175)

Madame Tussauds Selfie heaven, be it with Darth Vader or One Direction or the Queen. (p175)

MAZIARZ/SHUTTERSTOCK ©

Changing of the Guard
Soldiers in bearskin hats, red uniforms and military orders: kids will gape. (pictured above right; p58)

London Eye On many bucket lists, from tots to teens. (p135)

Hamleys A veritable wonderland awaits on the six floors of the world's oldest toy shop. (p84)

Best Museums

Science Museum Imaginative distractions for technical tykes and a fun-filled basement for little ones. (p156)

Imperial War Museum Packed with exciting displays, warplanes and military whatnot. (p134)

British Museum Meet the mummies at London's best museum. (p88)

Natural History Museum Gawp at the overhanging blue whale skeleton and animatronic T-rex. (p150)

Horniman Museum Fun aquarium and tons of hands-on exhibits. (p25)

Best for Babies & Toddlers

Kensington Gardens Fantastic playground, a fountain to splash about in, and hectares of greenery. (p160)

St James's Park Ducks, squirrels and pelicans. (p57)

Top Family Tips

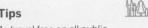

○ Under-11s travel free on all public transport, except National Rail services.

○ In winter months (November to January), ice rinks appear at the Natural History Museum, Somerset House, the Tower of London and Hampton Court.

Under the Radar London

HELEN CATHCART/LONELY PLANET ©

Park Life

The Covid-19 pandemic deepened London's appreciation for its beautiful green spaces. And as with its neighbourhoods, London's parks are plentiful and varied. Join locals admiring flowerbeds in a wrought-iron ringed garden inside a petite square of Georgian terraces, or sitting on a grassy slope watching the sunset behind apartment buildings, with British grime blaring from a nearby picnic.

Historic elements blend with modern life in London's parks: you may see a family feeding swans on an ornamental lake, a centuries-old Gothic-style water fountain, or walkers, roller-skaters and cyclists queuing at street-food stalls. On Victoria Park's southern border, a nomadic community lives in colourfully painted narrowboats with rooftop gardens. This is the London of everyday life.

Best Parkside Eats

Petersham Nurseries (www.petershamnurseries. com) Pre-book lunch at this Michelin green-starred restaurant (pictured) inside a flower-filled glasshouse before heading to Richmond Park.

Spaniards Inn (p181) Grab a Sunday roast at this 16th-century pub with an expansive beer garden opposite Hampstead Heath.

400 Rabbits (www.400 rabbits.co.uk) Serving sourdough pizza and housemade gelato from the lido cafe at Brixton's Brockwell Park.

The Glasshouse (www. glasshouserestaurant.co.uk) After roaming the majestic Kew Gardens, reward yourself with a seasonal dinner by the innovative British chef Gregory Wellman at this Michelin-starred locals' favourite.

Pavilion Bakery (www. pavilionbakery.com) Croissants, pastries and oat-milk coffee are the perfect treats for strolling Victoria Park's broad tree-lined avenue.

Festivals & Events

London is a vibrant city year-round, celebrating both traditional and modern festivals and events with energy and gusto. From Europe's largest outdoor carnival to the blooms of the Chelsea Flower Show and the pomp and ceremony of Trooping the Colour, London has entrancing and fascinating occasions for all tastes.

PRETTYAWESOME/SHUTTERSTOCK ©

Best Free Festivals

Notting Hill Carnival (www.thelondonnottinghillcarnival.com) London's most vibrant outdoor carnival is a celebration of Caribbean London; in August.

Trooping the Colour The Queen's official birthday in June sees parades and pageantry at the Horse Guards Parade.

Guy Fawkes' Night (Bonfire Night) Commemorates Guy Fawkes' attempt to blow up parliament in 1605, with bonfires and fireworks on 5 November.

Lord Mayor's Show (www.lordmayorsshow.org) Floats, bands and fireworks to celebrate the Lord Mayor in November.

Chinese New Year Chinatown fizzes in this colourful street festival in late January or February.

London Marathon Around 40,000 runners pound through London in April.

Best Ticketed Events

Wimbledon (www.wimbledon.com) Centre of the tennis universe for two weeks in June/July.

The Proms (www.bbc.co.uk/proms) Classical concerts around the Royal Albert Hall from July to September.

London Film Festival (www.bfi.org.uk/lff) Premier film event held at the BFI Southbank and other venues in October.

Chelsea Flower Show (pictured; www.rhs.org.uk/chelsea) Renowned horticultural show in May.

New Year On 31 December the countdown to midnight with Big Ben is met with fireworks from the London Eye. Buy tickets for the best view from www.london.gov.uk.

Events Listings Online

For a list of events in and around London, check www.visitlondon.com or www.timeout.com/london.

LGBTIQ+ London

The city of Oscar Wilde, Quentin Crisp and Elton John won't disappoint its gay visitors, offering a fantastic mix of brash, camp, loud and edgy parties, bars, clubs and events year-round. It's a world capital of gaydom, on par with New York and San Francisco – London's gay and lesbian communities have turned good times into an art form.

MARIUSZ GALAS/SHUTTERSTOCK ©

By Location

Fashionable Shoreditch is home to London's more alternative gay scene, often well mixed with local straight people. The long-established gay village of Soho has lost ground to edgy East End. Vauxhall in South London is where to go for the biggest club nights.

Bars & Clubs

Several famous venues have closed their doors in recent years – due, in part, to gentrification of traditionally gay neighbourhoods. That said, London still has a varied bar scene with venues citywide, not just in the traditional Soho heartland.

Best Clubs & Shops

Heaven Long-standing gay club and still a Saturday-night magnet. (p81)

Gay's the Word Excellent range of LGBTIQ-interest books and magazines, plus frequent events. (p104)

Best Events

BFI Flare (www.bfi.org.uk/llgff) Hosted by the BFI Southbank in early April, with premieres, screenings and talks.

Pride in London (pictured; www.prideinlondon.org) Huge gay-pride event in late June/early July.

LGBTIQ+ Event Listings

Check out www.facebook.com/GingerbeerUK for info on lesbian events, club nights and bars. Visit www.timeout.com/london/lgbt for bar, club and events listings.

Markets

SUN_SHINE/SHUTTERSTOCK ©

London Life

Shopping at London's markets isn't just about picking up bargains and rummaging through mounds of knick-knacks – although they give you plenty of opportunity to do that. It's also about taking in the character of this vibrant city: Londoners love to trawl through markets, browsing, chatting and socialising.

Lunch on the Side

Food stalls and/or food trucks are a feature of London markets, whether or not the markets specialise in food.

They generally do a roaring trade, thanks to hungry shoppers keen to sit and take in the buzz. The quality varies, but is generally good, and the prices are reasonable (£4 to £8).

Best Markets

Borough Market Bustling cornucopia of gastronomic delights, south of the river. (pictured; p134)

Old Spitalfields Market Huge, sprawling market on the border of the City and the East End, excellent for vintage and fashion. (p191)

Camden Market North London's must-see market. (p174)

Portobello Road Market London's best-known market, in ever-hip Notting Hill. (p167)

Brick Lane Market Sunday confluence of bric-a-brac, cheap clothes and street eats. (p185)

Sampling Borough Market

Look out for the plentiful freebie snack samples at Borough Market south of the river. The quality is top-notch and the variety of flavours breathtaking. Remember that the market simply heaves on Saturdays, so arrive early for the best pickings.

Four Perfect Days

Day 1

THE PICTURE STUDIO/SHUTTERSTOCK ©

First stop, **Trafalgar Sq** (p74) for its architecture, and the **National Gallery** (p66) for its superb art. Walk down Whitehall past **Downing St** (p58) to arrive at the **Houses of Parliament** (p50) and Big Ben. **Westminster Abbey** (p44) is nearby.

For gourmet cuisine at budget prices, lunch at **Vincent Rooms** (p59). Cross Westminster Bridge to the **London Eye** (pictured above; p135), then stroll South Bank to the **Tate Modern** (p128). Admire views of St Paul's from the **Millennium Bridge** (p137) and don't overlook **Shakespeare's Globe** (p141).

Enjoy a drink in the venerable **George Inn** (p141) and dinner at **Arabica Bar & Kitchen** (p137) in the historic **Borough Market** (p134).

Day 2

R CLASSEN/SHUTTERSTOCK ©

Get to the **Tower of London** (p112) early for the Unlocking of the Tower and follow the beefeaters to marvel at the Crown Jewels. Then admire iconic **Tower Bridge** (pictured above; p120) on the Thames. Head to **St Paul's** (p108) to lunch in its atmospheric crypt before exploring the architecture and dome. Take a bus to Covent Garden to feel the **piazza** (p72) buzz and watch street performers. Continue to **Piccadilly Circus** (p76) and its famous statue.

Stop by **Dukes London** (p60) for a relaxing Martini, followed by Israeli cuisine at **Palomar** (p77) or Italian at **Cafe Murano** (p53). Stay in Piccadilly and Soho for cocktails at **Rivoli Bar** (p60), or sink a welcome pint at **Lamb & Flag** (p80).

Day 3

WILF KOHNHAUS/SHUTTERSTOCK ©

Spend two hours at the **British Museum** (p88): join a tour of the permanent collection, listen to a gallery talk or explore on your own. Then stroll around **Bloomsbury** (p92), once the centre of the literary world.

Enjoy a sandwich at **Tea & Tattle** (p89), before heading to Chelsea and Kensington to (window) shop. **Harrods** (p165) is a must for gourmet souvenirs, while the shop at the **Victoria & Albert Museum** (p146) is great for gifts. End with a stroll around **Hyde Park** (pictured above; p157) or explore the **Natural History Museum** (p150).

Consider dinner at **Launceston Place** (p162), while for drinks the **Queen's Arms** (p151), **K Bar** (p164) or the **Windsor Castle** (p164) are all superb.

Day 4

WOLLERTZ/SHUTTERSTOCK ©

Take a boat from central London down the Thames to Greenwich for a historic **Greenwich walk** (p196). Explore the National Maritime Museum, Queen's House and the Cutty Sark. **Greenwich Market** (pictured above; p197) can sort lunch, with its abundant street food.

Stroll through **Greenwich Park** (p195) up to the **Royal Observatory** (p192). The views unfolding below you to Canary Wharf are magnificent. Inside the observatory, straddle the **Greenwich Meridian** (p193). Don't overlook the **Camera Obscura** (p193) and, at the **Weller Astronomy Galleries** (p195), touch something 4.5 billion years old!

Return to the river for a pint and dinner at the **Trafalgar Tavern** (p197).

Need to Know

For detailed information, see Survival Guide (p203)

Language
English

Currency
Pound sterling (£)

Visas
Not required for Australian, Canadian, NZ and US visitors, among others, for stays of up to six months.

Money
ATMs are widespread. Major credit cards are accepted everywhere.

Mobile Phones
Consider a local SIM card from a mobile network provider.

Time
London is on GMT/UTC.

Tipping
Hotels: £1 per bag. Pubs: never at the bar. Restaurants: service charge often included in bills, otherwise add 10% for decent service. Taxis: round the fare up to the nearest pound.

Daily Budget

Budget: Less than £85

Dorm bed: £12–30

Market-stall lunch or supermarket sandwich: £3.50–5

Many museums: free

Standby theatre tickets: 10p–£25

Santander Cycles daily rental fee: £2

Midrange: £85–200

Double room: £100–200

Two-course dinner with glass of wine: £35

Temporary exhibitions: £12–18

Theatre tickets: £15–60

Top end: More than £200

Four-star or boutique hotel room: from £200

Three-course dinner in top restaurant with wine: £60–90

Black-cab trip: £30

Top theatre tickets: £65

Advance Planning

Three months before Book accommodation, dinner reservations, and tickets for top shows and must-see temporary exhibitions.

One month before Check websites such as *Time Out* (www.timeout.com/london) for fringe theatre, live music and festivals, and book tickets.

A few days before Check the weather online through the Met Office (www.metoffice.gov.uk).

Arriving in London

Most people arrive in London by air, but an increasing number of visitors coming from Europe take the train.

✈ From Heathrow Airport

Trains, the Tube and buses to London from just after 5am to before midnight (night buses run later and 24-hour Tube runs Friday and Saturday) cost £5.10 to £25; a taxi will cost £50 to £100. The Heathrow Express train (£25) runs to Paddington train station.

✈ From Gatwick Airport

Trains to London from 4.30am to 1.35am cost £10 to £20; hourly buses to London run 24/7 and cost from £10; a taxi will cost £100.

✈ From Stansted Airport

Trains to London from 5.30am to 12.30am cost £19.40; 24/7 buses to London cost £7 to £10; a taxi will cost from £130.

✈ From Luton Airport

Trains to London from 7am to 10pm from £16.70; buses 24/7 to London, £7 to £11; taxi £110.

🚆 From St Pancras International Train Station

For Eurostar train arrivals from Europe, St Pancras is located in Central London and is connected by many underground lines to other parts of the city.

Getting Around

The cheapest way to get around London is with an Oyster Card (p209) or a UK contactless card (foreign cardholders should check for contactless charges first).

Ⓤ Tube, Overground & DLR

The London Underground ('the Tube'), Overground and DLR are, overall, the quickest ways to get around, if not the cheapest. Selected lines run all night on Friday and Saturday.

🚌 Bus

The bus network is extensive but slow-going except for short hops. Fares are good value with an Oyster or contactless card; plentiful night buses and 24-hour routes.

🚗 Taxi

Black-cab fares are steep unless you're in a group. Minicabs are cheaper. Apps such as Gett (for black cabs) and Bolt (for minicabs) are handy.

🚲 Bicycle

Santander Cycles are ideal for shorter journeys around central London.

🏍 Car & Motorcycle

As a visitor, it's unlikely you'll need to drive in London. Disincentives include steep parking charges, congestion charges, traffic jams, high petrol prices, diligent traffic wardens and wheel clamps.

London Neighbourhoods

Regent's Park & Camden (p169)
North London has a strong accent on nightlife, parkland and heaths, canal-side charm, markets and international menus.

National Gallery & Covent Garden (p65)
Bright lights, big city: West End theatres, big-ticket museums, fantastic restaurants, shopping galore and boho nightlife.

Natural History Museum

Buckingham Palace

Victoria & Albert Museum

Kensington Museums (p145)
One of London's classiest neighbourhoods with fine museums, hectares of parkland and top-grade shopping and dining.

Westminster Abbey & Westminster (p43)
The royal and political heart of London: pomp, pageantry and history in spades, and home to a number of London's biggest attractions.

British Museum & Bloomsbury (p87)
London's most famous museum, elegant squares, eclectic dining and literary pubs.

Shoreditch & the East End (p183)
London's creative and clubbing energy fills Shoreditch with history, museums, ace eats and markets aplenty in the East End.

British Museum ◉

National Gallery ◉◉

◉ **St Paul's Cathedral**

◉ **Tate Modern**

◉ **Tower of London**

◉◉ **Houses of Parliament**

Westminster Abbey

St Paul's & City of London (p107)
London's iconic church and tower are here, alongside ancient remains, historic churches, architectural gems and hearty pubs.

Tate Modern & South Bank (p127)
Modern art, innovative theatre, Elizabethan drama, superb dining, cutting-edge architecture and warmly traditional pubs.

◉ **Royal Observatory & Greenwich Park**

Explore
London

Worth a Trip 👀

London skyline _ULTRAFORMA_/GETTY IMAGES ©

Explore
Westminster Abbey & Westminster

Westminster is the political heart of London, and the level of pomp and circumstance here is astounding – state occasions are marked by convoys of gilded carriages, elaborate parades and, in the case of the opening of parliament, by a man in a black coat banging on the front door with a jewelled sceptre. Tourists flock here to marvel at Buckingham Palace and the neo-Gothic Houses of Parliament.

The Short List

○ **Westminster Abbey (p44)** *Admiring London's church for coronations, royal burials and weddings.*

○ **Buckingham Palace (p48)** *Visiting the Queen's official London residence in summer, or watching the ceremonious Changing of the Guard.*

○ **Houses of Parliament (p50)** *Touring the corridors of power in the spectacular Palace of Westminster.*

○ **Tate Britain (p56)** *Taking a walk through Britain's artistic heritage.*

○ **Churchill War Rooms (p56)** *Exploring Britain's underground bunker for WWII strategy.*

Getting There & Around

Ⓤ Westminster and St James's Park are both on the Circle and District Lines. The Jubilee Line runs through Westminster and Green Park; the latter station is also a stop on the Piccadilly and Victoria Lines.

Neighbourhood Map on p54

Big Ben & Houses of Parliament (p50) ALEXEY FEDORENKO/SHUTTERSTOCK ©

Top Experience 📷

Visit Kings and Queens at Westminster Abbey

Westminster Abbey is such an important commemoration site that it's hard to imagine its equivalent anywhere else in the world. Except for Edward V (murdered) and Edward VIII (abdicated), every English sovereign has been crowned here since William the Conqueror in 1066. Sixteen royals have been married here and many are buried here.

◉ MAP P54, E5

📞 020-7222 5152

www.westminster-abbey.org

20 Dean's Yard

adult/child £24/10, half-price from 4.30pm Wed

🕙 9.30am-3.30pm Mon, Tue, Thu & Fri, to 6pm Wed, to 3pm Sat

Ⓤ Westminster

North Transept, Sanctuary & Quire

The North Transept is often referred to as Statesmen's Aisle: politicians (notably prime ministers) and eminent public figures are commemorated by large marble statues and imposing marble plaques here. At the heart of the Abbey is the beautifully tiled sanctuary (or sacrarium), a stage for coronations, royal weddings and funerals. The Quire, a magnificent structure of gold, blue and red Victorian Gothic by Edward Blore, dates from the mid-19th century.

Lady Chapel & Coronation Chair

The spectacular Lady Chapel has a fan-vaulted ceiling, colourful heraldic banners and oak stalls. Behind the chapel's altar is the elaborate sarcophagus of Henry VII and his queen, Elizabeth of York. Opposite the entrance to the Lady Chapel is the Coronation Chair, seat of coronation for almost every monarch since the early 14th century.

Tomb of Mary Queen of Scots

There are two small chapels on either side of the Lady Chapel. On the left (north) is where Elizabeth I and her half-sister Mary I (or 'Bloody Mary') rest. On the right (south) is the tomb of Mary Queen of Scots, beheaded on the orders of her cousin Elizabeth in 1587.

Shrine of St Edward the Confessor

The most sacred spot in the abbey lies behind the High Altar, where access is generally restricted to protect the 13th-century floor. St Edward was the founder of the Abbey and the original building was consecrated a few weeks before his death. His tomb was slightly altered after the original was destroyed during the Reformation.

★ Top Tips

o Crowds are almost as solid as the Abbey's stonework, so buy tickets online in advance (which also nets a slight discount) or get in the queue first thing in the morning.

o Join one of the 1½-hour tours led by vergers (£7 plus admission) for a more in-depth look than the audio guide provides.

o Views from the Queen's Diamond Jubilee Galleries are the best in the building.

o Grab something to eat and use the toilet before entering; the cafe and toilets are at the end of the roped route, and it can be hard to get back to where you left off.

✕ Take a Break

Not far from the Abbey, the Vincent Rooms (p59), operated by the talented hospitality students of Westminster Kingsway College, is an excellent spot for modern European cuisine at very reasonable prices.

Poets' Corner

The south transept contains the Poets' Corner, where many of England's finest writers are buried and/or commemorated. The first poet to be buried here was Geoffrey Chaucer, joined later by Lord Alfred Tennyson, Charles Dickens, Robert Browning, Rudyard Kipling and other greats.

Sir Isaac Newton's Tomb

On the western side of the cloister is the Scientists' Corner, where you will find Sir Isaac Newton's tomb. A nearby section of the northern aisle of the nave is known as Musicians' Aisle, where baroque composers Henry Purcell and John Blow are buried, as well as more modern music makers such as Benjamin Britten and Edward Elgar.

Cloisters

Providing access to the monastic buildings, the quadrangular Cloisters – dating largely from the 13th to 15th centuries – would have once been a very active part of the Abbey and busy with monks. The Cloisters also provide access to the Chapter House, the Pyx Chamber and the Abbey Museum, situated in the vaulted undercroft.

Chapter House

The octagonal Chapter House has one of Europe's best-preserved medieval tile floors and retains traces of religious murals. Used as a meeting place by the House of Commons in the second half of the 14th century,

it also boasts what is claimed to be the oldest door in the UK – it's been there for 950 years.

Pyx Chamber

Next to the Chapter House and off the east cloister, the Pyx Chamber is one of the few remaining relics of the original Abbey and contains the Abbey's treasures and liturgical objects. Note the enormous trunks, which were made inside the room and used to store valuables from the Exchequer.

College Garden

To reach the 900-year-old College Garden (open 10am to 4pm Tuesday to Thursday), enter Little Dean's Yard and the Little Cloisters off Great College St. It occupies the site of the Abbey's first infirmary garden for cultivating medicinal herbs, established in the 11th century.

Queen's Diamond Jubilee Galleries

Opened in 2018, the Queen's Diamond Jubilee Galleries are a new museum and gallery space located in the medieval triforium, the arched gallery above the nave. Its exhibits include the death masks of generations of royalty, wax effigies representing Charles II and William III (who is on a stool to make him as tall as his wife, Mary II), armour and stained glass. Highlights are the graffiti-inscribed Mary Chair (used for the coronation of Mary II) and the 13th-century Westminster Retable, England's oldest altarpiece.

History of Westminster Abbey

Although a mixture of architectural styles, Westminster Abbey is considered the finest example of Early English Gothic (1190–1300). The original church was built in the 11th century by King (later St) Edward the Confessor, who is buried in the chapel behind the High Altar. Henry III (r 1216–72) began work on the new building, but didn't complete it; the French Gothic nave was finished in 1388. Henry VII's huge and magnificent chapel was added in 1519.

Benedictine Monastery & Dissolution

The Abbey was initially a monastery for Benedictine monks. Many of the building's features (the octagonal Chapter House, the Quire and Cloisters) attest to this collegial past. In 1534 Henry VIII separated the Church of England from the Catholic Church and proceeded to dissolve the country's monasteries. The King became head of the Church of England and the Abbey acquired its 'royal peculiar' status (administered directly by the Crown and exempt from any ecclesiastical jurisdiction).

Site of Coronation

With the exception of Edward V and Edward VIII, every English sovereign since William the Conqueror (in 1066) has been crowned here, and most of the monarchs from Henry III (died 1272) to George II (1760) were also buried here.

The Quire

The Quire dates back to the mid-19th century. It sits where the original choir for the monks' worship would have been but bears little resemblance to the original. Nowadays, the Quire is still used for singing, but its regular occupants are the Choir of Westminster Abbey – about 30 boys and 12 'lay vicars' (men) who sing the daily services and evensong (5pm on weekdays except Wednesday and 3pm on weekends).

Royal Wedding

On 29 April 2011 Prince William married Catherine Middleton at Westminster Abbey. The couple had chosen the Abbey for the relatively intimate setting of the Sanctuary – because of the Quire, three-quarters of the 1900-or-so guests couldn't see a thing! William and Kate's elaborately scrawled marriage certificate is now on display in the Queen's Diamond Jubilee Galleries.

Top Experience 📷
Wave to Royalty at Buckingham Palace

Built in 1703 for the Duke of Buckingham and then purchased by King George III, the palace has been the Royal Family's London lodgings since 1837 when Queen Victoria moved in. Commoners can get a peek at the State Rooms – a mere 19 of the palace's 775 rooms – from mid-July to September when Her Royal Highness is on holiday in Scotland.

◎ MAP P54, B4

☎ 0303 123 7300

www.rct.uk/visit/the-state-rooms-buckingham-palace

Buckingham Palace Rd

adult/child/under 5yr £26.50/14.50/free

🕙 9am-6pm mid-Jul–Sep

Ⓤ Green Park or St James's Park

State Rooms

The tour starts in the Grand Hall at the foot of the Grand Staircase, takes in John Nash's Italianate Green Drawing Room, the State Dining Room, the Blue Drawing Room (with a fluted ceiling by Nash) and the White Drawing Room, where foreign ambassadors are received. The Throne Room is rather anticlimactic, with his-and-her pink chairs monogrammed 'ER' and 'P'.

Picture Gallery & Gardens

The 47m-long Picture Gallery has splendid works by such artists as Van Dyck, Rubens, Rembrandt, Canaletto, Poussin, Canova and Vermeer. Wandering the 16 hectares of gardens after the tour is another highlight, as well as admiring some of the 350 or so species of plants.

Queen's Gallery

The Royal Family has amassed a priceless collection of paintings, sculpture, ceramics, furniture and jewellery. The splendid **Queen's Gallery** (South Wing, Buckingham Palace; adult/child £13.50/6.70; ⊙10am-5.30pm, from 9.30am mid-Jul–Sep) showcases some of the palace's treasures on a rotating basis. Entrance to the gallery is from Buckingham Gate.

Royal Mews

Southwest of the palace, the **Royal Mews** (Buckingham Palace Rd; adult/child £13/7.50; ⊙10am-5pm Apr-Oct, to 4pm Mon-Sat Feb, Mar & Nov; ⓤVictoria) started life as a falconry but is now a working stable looking after the royals' immaculately groomed horses, along with the opulent vehicles the monarch uses for transport. Highlights include the magnificent Gold State Coach of 1762, and the 1911 Glass Coach.

★ Top Tips

o Entry to the palace is by timed ticket (departures every quarter-hour), which must be booked online. The self-guided tour (audio guide included) takes about two hours.

o A Royal Day Out (adult/child/under five years £49/26.50/free) is a combined ticket including entry to the State Rooms, Queen's Gallery and Royal Mews.

o The Changing of the Guard (p58) is very popular; arrive early to secure a good view.

✕ Take a Break

Make a booking at the Other Naughty Piglet (p59) for a fixed-price lunch menu (two courses £18) of small-plate-style dining in this open-plan bistro, inside the Other Palace Theatre. Fish, meat and wine are all strong features of the seasonal menu.

Top Experience 📷

Walk the Stately Houses of Parliament

Both the elected House of Commons and the House of Lords, who are appointed or hereditary, sit in the sumptuous Palace of Westminster, a neo-Gothic confection dating from the mid-19th century (with a few sections that survived a catastrophic fire in 1834). A visit here is a journey to the very heart of British democracy.

◎ MAP P54, F5

☏ tours 020-7219 4114

www.parliament.uk

Parliament Sq

guided tour adult/child £26.50/11.50, audio-guide tour £19.50/free

Ⓤ Westminster

Big Ben

The most famous feature of the Houses of Parliament is the Clock Tower, officially named the Elizabeth Tower to mark the Queen's Diamond Jubilee in 2012 but commonly known as Big Ben. Big Ben is actually the 13.5-tonne bell hanging inside and is named after Benjamin Hall, the first Commissioner of Works when the tower was completed in 1859.

Westminster Hall

One of the most interesting features of the monumental Palace of Westminster, seat of the English monarchy from the 11th to the early 16th centuries, is Westminster Hall. Originally built at the end of the 11th century, it is the oldest surviving part of the complex; the awesome hammer-beam roof was added between 1393 and 1401.

House of Commons

The House of Commons is where Members of Parliament (MPs) meet to propose and discuss new legislation and to grill the prime minister and other ministers. The chamber, designed by Giles Gilbert Scott, replaced the one destroyed by a 1941 bomb.

House of Lords

The House of Lords is visited via the amusingly named Strangers' Gallery. The intricate 'Tudor Gothic' interior led its architect, Auguste Pugin (1812–52), to an early death from overwork and nervous strain.

Tours

Visitors are welcome on either guided or self-guided tours on Saturdays year-round and on most weekdays during parliamentary recesses.

★ **Top Tips**

o Book tours in advance. Not only are prices cheaper but because they often happen only once a week (on Saturdays), they also fill up quickly.

o Stay for afternoon tea to continue soaking up the splendour.

✕ **Take a Break**

Take afternoon tea in a riverside House of Commons room for an additional £30 (£15 for children). The House of Commons Members' Dining Room is sometimes open to the public, too.

Better yet, consider booking lunch at the elegant Skylon (p138) in Southbank Centre with floor-to-ceiling window views of the Thames and skyline.

Walking Tour 🚶

Royal London

Lassoing the cream of London's royal and stately sights, this attraction-packed walk ticks off some of the city's truly must-do experiences on one comprehensive route. You'll be passing some of London's most famous buildings and historic sites, so photo opportunities abound. The walk conveniently returns you in a loop to your starting point for easy access to other parts of London.

Walk Facts

Start Westminster Abbey; Ⓤ Westminster

End Houses of Parliament; Ⓤ Westminster

Length 2.2 miles; two hours

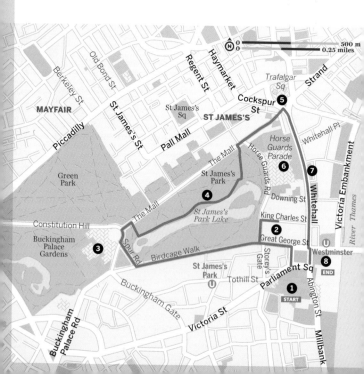

❶ Westminster Abbey

Start by exploring mighty Westminster Abbey (p44), preferably before the crowds arrive. Almost every English sovereign since 1066 has been crowned here.

❷ Churchill War Rooms

Walk around Parliament Sq, past the UK Supreme Court on the west side of the square, to the Churchill War Rooms (p56) to discover how Churchill coordinated the Allied war against Hitler.

❸ Buckingham Palace

Strolling to the end of Birdcage Walk brings you to majestic Buckingham Palace (p48), where the state rooms are accessible to ticket holders in August and September – or pay a visit to the nearby Royal Mews (p49) and the Queen's Gallery (p49).

❹ St James's Park

Amble along The Mall and enter St James's Park (p57), one of London's most attractive royal parks. Walk alongside St James's Park Lake for its plentiful ducks, geese, swans and other waterfowl.

❺ Trafalgar Square

Return to The Mall and pass through Admiralty Arch to the hubbub of Trafalgar Square (p74) and take in the regal views down Whitehall to the Houses of Parliament.

❻ Horse Guards Parade

Walk down Whitehall to the entrance to Horse Guards Parade (p58). The dashing mounted sentries of the Queen's Household Cavalry are on duty here daily from 10am to 4pm, when the dismounted guards are changed.

❼ Banqueting House

On the far side of the street, magnificent Banqueting House (p57) is the last surviving remnant of Whitehall Palace, which vanished in a late-17th-century fire. Further down Whitehall is the entrance to No 10 Downing St (p58).

❽ Houses of Parliament

At the end of Whitehall, you'll reach the magnificently Gothic Houses of Parliament (p50) and its famous tower, Big Ben. You can tour the building on a guided or self-directed audio tour.

✕ Take a Break

Pack a picnic to eat in lovely St James's Park (p57) if it's a sunny day. Alternatively, **Cafe Murano** (Map p54, B2; 📞020-3371 5559; www.cafemura no.co.uk; 33 St James's St; mains £18-28; ⏱noon-3pm & 5.30-11pm Mon-Sat, 11.30am-4pm Sun; Ⓤ Green Park) in the nearby neighbourhood of St James's is a fine choice for authentic cuisine from northern Italy.

Westminster Abbey & Westminster

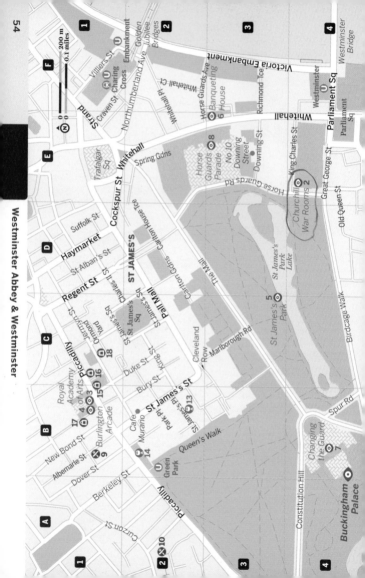

F
200 m
0.1 miles
N

1
Villiers St
Charing Cross Embankment U
Golden Jubilee Bridges
Craven St
Strand
Northumberland Ave

2
Whitehall Ct
Whitehall Pl
Horse Guards Ave
Banqueting House 6
Richmond Tce
Victoria Embankment

3
Whitehall
Westminster U
King Charles St
Parliament Sq

4
Parliament Sq
Westminster Bridge
Great George St
Old Queen St

Suffolk St
Haymarket
St Alban's St
Regent St
ST JAMES'S
Spring Gdns
Horse Guards Parade 8
No 10 Downing Street
Downing St
Horse Guards Rd
Churchill War Rooms 2

D
Trafalgar Sq
Cockspur St Whitehall

E
Carlton House Tce
Carlton Gdns
The Mall
St James's Park Lake
St James's Park 5

Royal Academy of Arts Piccadilly
17 4 3 15 16
Burlington Arcade
18
Jermyn St
Ormond Yard
St James's Sq
St James's St
Charles II St
Pall Mall
King St
Duke St
Bury St
Cleveland Row
Marlborough Rd

New Bond St
Albemarle St
Dover St
9
Café Murano
14
St James's St
Park Pl
13
Queen's Walk
Green Park U
Piccadilly
Berkeley St
Curzon St

2 10

Buckingham Palace
Changing the Guard 7
Spur Rd
Constitution Hill
Birdcage Walk

A **B** **C** **D** **E** **F**
1 **2** **3** **4**

Westminster Abbey & Westminster

Houses of Parliament

River Thames

Lambeth Bridge

Millbank

Tate Britain ◎ 10 Atterbury St

Abington St

Millbank

Victoria Tower Gardens

Westminster Abbey

Great College St

Tufton St

Marsham St

Johnsons St

Herrick St

Erasmus St

Dean's Yard

Great Smith St

Marsham St

WESTMINSTER

Page St

Vincent St

Horseferry Rd

Victoria St

Tothill St

Monck St

Great Peter St

Old Pye St

Medway St

Chadwick St

Regency St

Chapter St

Douglas St

Hide Pl

Vincent St

Vauxhall Bridge Rd

St James's Park

Broadway

Petty France

Caxton St

Greycoat Pl

Greycoat

Elverton St

Maunsel St

Vincent St

12 ✗

Rochester Row

Greencoat Pl

Francis St

Stillington St

Willow Pl

Vincent Sq

Vincent Sq

Charlwood St

Belgrave Rd

Buckingham Gate

Wilfred St

Castle La

Palace St

Cardinal Walk

Victoria St

Howick Pl

Ashley Pl

Morpeth Tce

Carlisle Pl

Vauxhall Bridge Rd

Warwick Way

Bressenden Pl

✗ 11

Bridge Pl

Gillingham St

Wilton Rd

Victoria St

Victoria ◎ ⊍

Wilton Rd

Buckingham Palace Rd

For reviews see

Sights

Tate Britain
GALLERY

1 ⊙ MAP P54, E8

On the site of the former Millbank Penitentiary, the older and more venerable of the two Tate siblings opened in 1892 and celebrates British art from 1500 to the present, including pieces from William Blake, William Hogarth, Thomas Gainsborough and John Constable, as well as vibrant modern and contemporary pieces from Lucian Freud, Barbara Hepworth, Gillian Ayres, Francis Bacon and Henry Moore. The stars of the show are, undoubtedly, the light-infused visions of JMW Turner in the Clore Gallery. (☎020-7887 8888; www.tate.org.uk/visit/tate-britain; Millbank; admission free; ⊙10am-6pm; Ⓤ Pimlico)

Churchill War Rooms
MUSEUM

2 ⊙ MAP P54, E4

Former Prime Minister Winston Churchill helped coordinate the Allied resistance against Nazi Germany on a Bakelite telephone from this underground complex during WWII. The Cabinet War Rooms remain much as they were when the lights were switched off in 1945, capturing the drama and dogged spirit of the time, while the modern multimedia Churchill Museum affords intriguing insights into the life and times of the resolute wartime leader. (☎020-7416 5000; www.iwm.org.uk; Clive Steps, King Charles St; adult/child £23/11.50; ⊙9.30am-6pm; Ⓤ Westminster)

Royal Academy of Arts
GALLERY

3 ⊙ MAP P54, B1

Britain's oldest society devoted to fine arts was founded in 1768 and moved here to Burlington House a century later. For its 250th birthday in 2018, the RA gave itself a £56-million makeover, including a magnificent expansion into 6 Burlington Gardens. Its collection of drawings, paintings, architectural designs, photographs and sculptures by past and present Royal Academicians, such as Sir Joshua Reynolds, John Constable, Thomas Gainsborough, JMW Turner, David Hockney and Tracey Emin, has historically been male-dominated, but this is slowly changing. (☎020-7300 8000; www.royalacademy.org.uk; Burlington House, Piccadilly; admission free; ⊙10am-6pm Sat-Thu, to 10pm Fri; Ⓤ Green Park)

Burlington Arcade
HISTORIC BUILDING

4 ⊙ MAP P54, B1

Flanking Burlington House, which is home to the Royal Academy of Arts, is this delightful arcade, built in 1819. Today it is a shopping precinct for the wealthy, and is most famous for the Burlington Beadles, uniformed guards who patrol the area keeping an eye out for such offences as running, chewing gum, whistling, opening umbrellas or anything else that could lower the tone. (The fact that the arcade once served as a brothel is kept quiet.)

CHRISPICTURES/SHUTTERSTOCK ©

Royal Academy of Arts

Running perpendicular to Burlington Arcade between Old Bond and Albermarle Sts is the more recent 1880 Royal Arcade. (www.burlingtonarcade.com; 51 Piccadilly; ⊙9am-7.30pm Mon-Sat, 11am-6pm Sun; Ⓤ Green Park)

St James's Park PARK

5 ◉ MAP P54, C3

At 23 hectares, St James's is the second-smallest of the eight royal parks after **Green Park** (www.royalparks.org.uk/parks/green-park; ⊙5am-midnight; Ⓤ Green Park). But what it lacks in size it makes up for in grooming, as it is the most manicured green space in London. It has brilliant views of the London Eye, Westminster, St James's Palace, Carlton House Terrace and Horse Guards Parade; the

picture-perfect sight of Buckingham Palace from the Blue Bridge spanning the central lake is the best you'll find. (www.royalparks.org.uk/parks/st-jamess-park; The Mall; ⊙5am-midnight; Ⓤ St James's Park or Green Park)

Banqueting House PALACE

6 ◉ MAP P54, E3

Banqueting House is the sole surviving section of the Tudor Whitehall Palace (1532) that once stretched most of the way down Whitehall before burning to the ground in a 1698 conflagration. Designed by Inigo Jones in 1622 and refaced in Portland stone in the 19th century, Banqueting House was England's first purely Renaissance building and resembled no other structure in

No 10 Downing Street

The official office of British leaders since 1735, when George II presented No 10 to 'First Lord of the Treasury' Robert Walpole, **No 10 Downing Street** (Map p54, E3; www.number10.gov.uk; 10 Downing St; U Westminster) has also been the prime minister's London residence since refurbishment in 1902. For such a famous address, No 10 is a small-looking Georgian building on a plain-looking street, hardly warranting comparison with the White House, for example. Yet it is actually three houses joined into one and boasts roughly 100 rooms plus a 2000-sq-metre garden.

the country at the time. Don't miss the Undercroft cellar. (020-3166 6000; www.hrp.org.uk/banqueting-house; Whitehall; adult/child £7.50/free; 10am-5pm; U Westminster)

Changing the Guard   CEREMONY

 7 MAP P54, B4

The full-on pageantry of soldiers in bright-red uniforms and bearskin hats parading down the Mall and into Buckingham Palace (p48) is madly popular with tourists. The event lasts about 45 minutes and ends with a full military band playing music from traditional marches, musicals and pop songs. The pomp and circumstance can

feel far away indeed when you're in row 15, trying to watch the ceremony through a forest of selfie sticks. Get here at least 45 minutes before the main event. (www.royal.uk/changing-guard; Buckingham Palace, Buckingham Palace Rd; admission free; 11am Mon, Wed, Fri, Sun Aug-May, 11am daily Jun & Jul; U St James's Park or Green Park)

Horse Guards Parade   HISTORIC SITE

8 MAP P54, E3

In a more accessible version of Buckingham Palace's Changing the Guard, the horse-mounted troops of the Household Cavalry swap soldiers here at 11am from Monday to Saturday and at 10am on Sunday. A slightly less ceremonial version takes place at 4pm when the dismounted guards are changed. On the Queen's official birthday in June, the **Trooping the Colour** (www.householddivision.org.uk/trooping-the-colour) parade takes place here. (off Whitehall; U Westminster or Charing Cross)

Eating

Gymkhana   INDIAN £££

 9 MAP P54, B1

The rather sombre setting at this serious Indian fine-dining establishment is intended to invoke the 'good old days' of the British Raj – lazily whirling fans in oak ceilings, period cricket photos and hunting trophies – but the food is anything but dull. Seven-course tasting meat/vegetarian menus are offered (£85/80), and the bar, reminiscent of a 17th-century East India punch-house, opens until 1am. (☎020-3011 5900; www.gymkhanalondon.com; 42 Albemarle St; mains £17-38, 4-course menus £40; ⏱noon-2.30pm & 5.30-10.15pm Mon-Sat; 🛜🍴; Ⓤ Green Park)

Kitty Fisher's
MODERN BRITISH £££

10 ❌ MAP P54, A2

Taking pride of place in Mayfair's 18th-century Shepherd Market (historically one of London's red-light districts), this cosy dining room is named after the 18th-century courtesan painted by Joshua Reynolds. Now a handsomely furnished, twin-roomed restaurant, it serves quality British fare such as monkfish with cauliflower and curried butter, or partridge with celeriac and pickled pear. The wine list is excellent. (☎020-3302 1661; www.kittyfishers.com; 10 Shepherd Market; mains £27-29; ⏱noon-2.30pm & 6-9.30pm Mon-Sat; Ⓤ Green Park)

The Other Naughty Piglet
BISTRO ££

11 ❌ MAP P54, B5

On the first floor of the Other Palace Theatre and roomier than Naughty Piglets, its elder sibling in Brixton, this unpretentious open-kitchen restaurant is a pleasure, tempting with seasonally opportunistic dishes such as smoked eel, rhubarb, ginger and coriander. Lunch and pre-theatre set menus, offered Tuesday to Saturday, are great value (two/three courses £18/22). (☎020-7592 0322; www.theothernaughtypiglet.co.uk; The Other Palace Theatre, 12 Palace St; small plates £10-12; ⏱noon-2.15pm Tue-Sat & 5.15-9.15pm Mon-Sat; 🛜; Ⓤ Victoria)

Vincent Rooms
MODERN EUROPEAN ££

12 ❌ MAP P54, C7

Care to be a guinea pig for student chefs at Westminster Kingsway College, where such celebrity chefs as Jamie Oliver and Ainsley Harriott were trained? Service is eager to please, the atmosphere in both the Brasserie and the Escoffier Room smarter than expected, and the food (including veg options) ranges from wonderful to exquisite – at very affordable prices. (☎020-7802 8391; www.thevincentrooms.co.uk; Westminster Kingsway College, Vincent Sq; 2/3 courses £17/21; ⏱noon-3pm Mon-Fri & 6-9pm Tue-Thu in term time; Ⓤ Victoria)

Westminster Nightlife?

Westminster and Whitehall are fairly deserted in the evenings, with little in the way of bars or restaurants. It's pretty much the same story for St James's. Instead, head north to Soho for a vibrant concentration of bars, restaurants and live music, or across the Thames to South Bank's theatres, pubs and restaurants.

Dukes London

Drinking

Dukes London COCKTAIL BAR

13 MAP P54, B2

Superb martinis and a gentlemen's-club-like ambience are the ingredients of this classic bar, where white-jacketed masters mix up perfect preparations. James Bond fans should make a pilgrimage here: author Ian Fleming used to frequent the place, where he undoubtedly ordered his drinks 'shaken, not stirred'. Smokers can ease into the secluded Cognac and Cigar Garden to enjoy cigars purchased here. (☏020-7491 4840; www.dukeshotel. com/dukes-bar; Dukes Hotel, 35 St James's Pl; ⊙2-11pm Mon-Sat, 4-10.30pm Sun; 🛜; Ⓤ Green Park)

Rivoli Bar COCKTAIL BAR

14 MAP P54, B2

You may not quite need a diamond as big as the Ritz to drink at this art-deco marvel, but it might help. All camphor wood, illuminated La-lique glass, golden-ceiling domes and stunning cocktails, the bar is a gem. Unlike in some other parts of the Ritz, dress code here is smart casual (this laxity does not extend to trainers). Caviar, oysters, and more substantial classics such as tuna niçoise and oxtail shepherd's pie are available between 11.30am and 10.30pm (£36 to £375). (☏020-7493 8181; www.theritzlondon. com/dine-with-us/rivoli-bar; Ritz London, 150 Piccadilly; ⊙11.30am-11.30pm Mon-Sat, noon-10.30pm Sun; 🛜; Ⓤ Green Park)

Shopping

Fortnum & Mason
DEPARTMENT STORE

15 🔒 MAP P54, B1

With its classic eau-de-Nil (pale green) colour scheme, the 'Queen's grocery store' (established in 1707) refuses to yield to modern times. Its staff – men and women – still wear old-fashioned tailcoats, and its glamorous food hall is supplied with hampers, marmalade and speciality teas. Stop for a spot of afternoon tea at the Diamond Jubilee Tea Salon, visited by Queen Elizabeth II in 2012. (☎020-7734 8040; www.fortnumandmason.com; 181 Piccadilly; ◷10am-9pm Mon-Sat, 11.30am-6pm Sun; Ⓤ Green Park or Piccadilly Circus)

Hatchards
BOOKS

16 🔒 MAP P54, C1

The UK's oldest bookshop dates back to 1797, and has been cramped into this Georgian building for more than 200 years. Holding three royal warrants, Hatchards has a solid supply of signed editions plus a strong selection of first editions on the ground floor. (☎020-7439 9921; www.hatchards.co.uk; 187 Piccadilly; ◷9.30am-8pm Mon-Sat, noon-6.30pm Sun; Ⓤ Green Park or Piccadilly Circus)

Penhaligon's
PERFUME

17 🔒 MAP P54, B1

Follow your nose through the historic Burlington Arcade (p56) to this classic British perfumery. Attendants enquire about your favourite smells, take you on an exploratory tour of the shop's signature range, and help you discover new scents in their traditional perfumes, home fragrances and bath and body products. Everything is produced in England, with prices to match. (☎020-7629 1416; www.penhaligons.com; 16-17 Burlington Arcade; ◷9am-6.30pm Mon-Fri, from 9.30am Sat, noon-6pm Sun; Ⓤ Piccadilly Circus or Green Park)

Paxton & Whitfield
FOOD & DRINKS

18 🔒 MAP P54, C1

With modest beginnings as an Aldwych stall in 1742 and purveying a dizzying range of fine cheeses, this black- and gold-fronted shop holds two royal warrants. Whatever your cheese leanings, you'll find the shop well supplied with hard and soft cheeses as well as blue and washed-rind examples. (☎020-7930 0259; www.paxtonandwhitfield.co.uk; 93 Jermyn St; ◷10am-6.30pm Mon-Sat, 11am-5pm Sun; Ⓤ Piccadilly Circus or Green Park)

Walking Tour 🚶

Tower of London to the Tate Modern

Commencing at one of London's most historic sights, this walk crosses the Thames on magnificent Tower Bridge before heading west along the river, scooping up some excellent views and passing breathtaking modern architecture, history and Shakespeare's Globe on the way. It comes to a halt amid the renowned contemporary artworks of the Tate Modern.

Walk Facts

Start Tower of London;
Ⓤ Tower Hill

End Tate Modern;
Ⓤ Southwark

Length 2.2 miles;
1½ hours

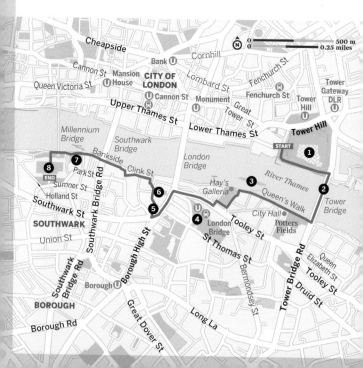

❶ Tower of London

The ancient Tower of London (p112) contains the oldest still-standing structure in the city, built in the 1070s. Be dazzled by the Crown Jewels, and tag along with a Yeoman Warder on an enlightening and entertaining tour.

❷ Tower Bridge

Cross ornate 19th-century Tower Bridge (p120) to the south side of the Thames. The bridge still raises, although these days it's powered electrically instead of by steam, and shuts down traffic mainly for pleasure craft.

❸ HMS Belfast

Head down the stairs and walk west along the riverside Queen's Walk past City Hall. Moored a bit further ahead, HMS Belfast (p136), a light cruiser that served in WWII and later conflicts, is a floating museum.

❹ Shard

Stroll through the enclosed-dock-turned-shopping-complex of Hay's Galleria to Tooley St to see the Shard (p136), one of the tallest buildings in Europe.

❺ Borough Market

Continue west along Tooley St and dip south to Borough Market (p134), overflowing with small shops, food stalls and wholesale greengrocers catering to London's top-end restaurants.

❻ Southwark Cathedral

Southwark Cathedral (p135) is both fascinating and relaxing. Parts of the church date to medieval times, but its interior is beautifully Gothic, lined with pointed arches down the long nave and a 16th-century saint-filled high altar screen.

❼ Shakespeare's Globe

Wander west along Clink St – and past the remains of Winchester Palace – to Bankside and on to Shakespeare's Globe (p141). Join one of the informative tours or book tickets for a later show.

❽ Tate Modern

About 100m west of Shakespeare's Globe is the elegant Millennium Bridge (p137) and London's standout modern- and contemporary-art gallery, the Tate Modern (p128).

✕ Take a Break

Borough Market's takeaway food stalls cluster in Green Market, close to Southwark Cathedral. Fill up on anything from sizzling gourmet German sausages to Ethiopian curries and Caribbean stews. For a sit-down meal, try one of the many restaurants on the market fringes, such as Arabica Bar & Kitchen (p137) and Padella (p137).

Explore

National Gallery & Covent Garden

At the centre of the West End – London's physical, cultural and social heart – the neighbourhood around the National Gallery and Covent Garden is a sightseeing hub. This is London's busiest neighbourhood, with a grand convergence of monumental history, stylish restaurants, standout entertainment choices and classic pubs. And if you're in town to shop, you'll be in seventh heaven.

The Short List

o **National Gallery (p66)** *Admiring masterpieces from Europe in this palatial gallery.*

o **Covent Garden (p72)** *Eating, drinking and being merry in a bustling piazza.*

o **Chinatown (p73)** *Browsing the thriving pedestrianised food and shopping district.*

o **Soho (p73)** *Strolling London's most infamous streets for eating, drinking and partying.*

o **Somerset House (p74)** *Watching films in summer and ice skating in winter.*

Getting There & Around

U Piccadilly Circus, Leicester Sq and Covent Garden (all on Piccadilly Line) or Leicester Sq, Charing Cross and Embankment (all on Northern Line).

Neighbourhood Map on p70

National Gallery (p66) JOE KUIS/SHUTTERSTOCK ©

Top Experience 📷
Catch Amazing Art at the National Gallery

With some 2300 European paintings on display, this is one of the world's richest art collections, with seminal paintings from the mid-13th to the early 20th century, including works by Leonardo da Vinci, Michelangelo, Titian, Van Gogh, Monet, Renoir and Rembrandt.

◎ MAP P70, E6

☎ 020-7747 2885

www.nationalgallery.org.uk

Trafalgar Sq

admission free

🕙 10am-6pm Sat-Thu, to 9pm Fri

Ⓤ Charing Cross

Sainsbury Wing

The Sainsbury Wing (1260–1510) houses plenty of fine religious paintings commissioned for private devotion, as well as more unusual masterpieces such as Botticelli's *Venus & Mars*. Leonardo da Vinci's *Virgin of the Rocks* (room 66) is a visual and technical masterpiece.

West & North Wings

Works from the High Renaissance embellish the West Wing (1500–1600) where Michelangelo, Titian, Raphael, Correggio, El Greco and Bronzino hold court; Rubens, Rembrandt and Caravaggio grace the North Wing (1600–1700). Notable here are two self-portraits of Rembrandt (at age 34 and at 63, in room 22) and the beautiful *Rokeby Venus* by Velázquez in room 30.

East Wing

The East Wing (1700–1930) has works by 18th-century British artists such as Gainsborough, Constable and Turner, and seminal Impressionist and post-Impressionist masterpieces by Van Gogh, Renoir and Monet await.

Rain, Steam & Speed: The Great Western Railway

In Room 34, this magnificent oil painting from Turner was created in 1844. Generally considered to depict the Maidenhead Railway Bridge, the painting reveals the forces reshaping the world at the time: railways, speed and a reinterpretation of the use of light, atmosphere and colour in art. Look for the dashing hare.

Sunflowers

In Room 45 hangs one of several sunflower still lifes painted by Van Gogh in late 1888; this masterpiece displays a variety of then-innovative artistic techniques, with the vividness of the colour conveying a powerful sense of affirmation.

★ Top Tips

○ Free one-hour guided tours leave from the Sainsbury Wing foyer at 2pm Monday to Friday.

○ If you want to go it alone, the audio guide (£5) is highly recommended.

○ There are special trails and activity sheets for children.

○ The gallery is open until 9pm on Friday.

✕ Take a Break

Historic Gordon's Wine Bar (p81) nearby serves cheese platters with its wines inside the cavernous candlelit interior or at sunny tables on Watergate Walk.

For a quicker bite, the **National Café** (☏020-7747 2525; ground fl, National Gallery; 2-/3-course set lunch £20/25; ⏱9.30am-8.30pm Mon-Thu, to 10pm Fri, to 6pm Sat & Sun) offers self-serve light meals as well as a proper sit-down bistro.

Walking Tour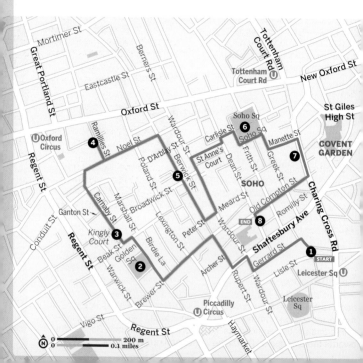

A Stroll Through Soho

Soho may come into its own in the evenings, but daytime guarantees other surprises and opportunities to be charmed by the area's bohemian leanings, diversity, creative energy and history. Thread your way from Chinatown through intriguing backstreets, genteel squares and markets to one of the neighbourhood's signature bars.

Walk Facts

Start Chinatown;
Ⓤ Leicester Sq

Finish French House Soho;
Ⓤ Leicester Sq

Length 1.2 miles;
three to six hours

❶ Chinatown

Just north of Leicester Sq Tube station are Lisle and Gerrard Sts, a focal point for London's Chinese community. A tight tangle of roast-duck shops, supermarkets and dim sum canteens, it's a vibrant spot for a bite to eat.

❷ Golden Square

North of Brewer St, historic Golden Sq (featured in Charles Dickens' *The Life and Adventures of Nicholas Nickleby*) was once part of an area called Windmill Fields. This lovely 17th-century square was probably Christopher Wren's design. The garden in the middle is a relaxing place with interesting (and often amusing) sculptures.

❸ Carnaby Street

Synonymous with the Swinging Sixties, London's subcultures have always congregated around Carnaby St. Today its colourful facades house an eclectic mix of designer and big-name brand stores. Between its street art and themed Christmas lights, it's hugely photogenic.

❹ Photographers' Gallery

The inspiring **Photographers' Gallery** (www.thephotographers gallery.org.uk; 16-18 Ramillies St; adult/child £5/free; ⏰10am-6pm Mon-Wed, Fri & Sat, to 8pm Thu, 11am-6pm Sun) has five floors of exhibition space, a cafe and a shop brimming with prints and photography books. It awards the prestigious Deutsche Börse Photography Prize, of considerable importance for contemporary photographers.

❺ Berwick Street

The vinyl revival is alive and well in neighbouring Berwick and Broadwick Sts. With some of London's best music stores, you'll be riffling through excellent back catalogues across genres from rock and soul to reggae and dubstep.

❻ Soho Square

Cut through tiny St Anne's Court to Dean St (where Karl Marx lived at No 28 from 1851 to 1856) and leafy Soho Sq (p73) where Londoners catch some sun on unclouday days. Laid out in 1681, it was originally named King's Sq (hence the statue of Charles II).

❼ Foyles

Is there a better way to while away an afternoon than at a bookstore? Foyles (p82), London's legendary bookshop, sells titles on every topic imaginable plus Grant & Cutler foreign-language titles on the 4th floor; an excellent cafe is on the 5th.

❽ French House

Walk down Old Compton St to Soho's legendary boozer, French House (p81), the meeting place of Free French Forces during WWII – de Gaulle is said to have drunk here, while Dylan Thomas, Peter O'Toole and Francis Bacon often ended up horizontal.

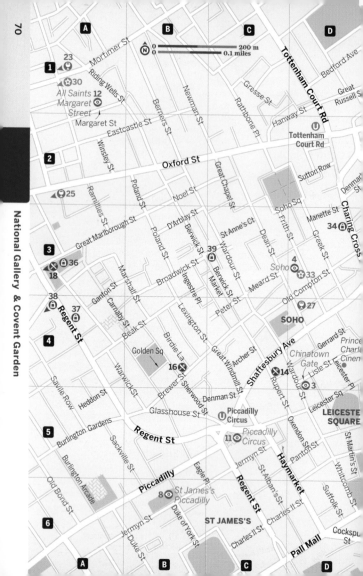

23 🔻🚇
1
⭐🚇**30**
All Saints **12** 🚇
Margaret
Street
Margaret St

Mortimer St
Riding Wells St
Newman St
Gresse St
Hanway St
Tottenham Court Rd 🚇
Tottenham
Court Rd
Bedford Ave
Great Russell S
Berners St
Rathbone Pl

Eastcastle St
Winsley St

2
Oxford St
Sutton Row
Denman

🔻🚇**25**
Ramillies St
Poland St
Noel St
Great Chapel St
Soho Sq
Frith St
Manette St
Charing Cross
Charing Cross

34 🔒

Great Marlborough St
D'Arblay St
Poland St
Berwick St
St Anne's Ct
Dean St
Greek St

3
🔻🚇**36**
18
Marshall St
Broadwick St
Ingestre Pl
Wardour St
Berwick St Market
Soho 🚇 **4**
🚇**33**
Meard St
Old Compton St

38 🔻🔒
37 🔒
Regent St
Ganton St
Carnaby St
Beak St
Lexington St
Peter St
🚇**27**
SOHO

4
Golden Sq
Birdie La
16 🚇
Great Windmill St
Archer St
Shaftesbury Ave
Chinatown Gate
Gerrard St
Prince Charle
Cinem
Wardour St
Lisle St
14 🔻
3
Leicester Sq
LEICESTE
SQUARE

Savile Row
Warwick St
Brewer St
Sherwood St
Denman St
Rupert St

5
Heddon St
Burlington Gardens
Sackville St
Glasshouse St
Regent St
Piccadilly Circus 🚇
11 🚇
Piccadilly Circus
Jermyn St
St Alban's St
Haymarket
Regent St
Panton St
Oxendon St
St Martin's St
Whitcomb St
Suffolk St

Old Bond St
Burlington Arcade
Piccadilly
Eagle Pl

6
Jermyn St
Duke St
Duke of York St
8 🚇
St James's Piccadilly
ST JAMES'S
Charles St
Charles II St
Charles II St
Pall Mall
Cockspu
St

N 0 — 200 m
0 — 0.1 miles

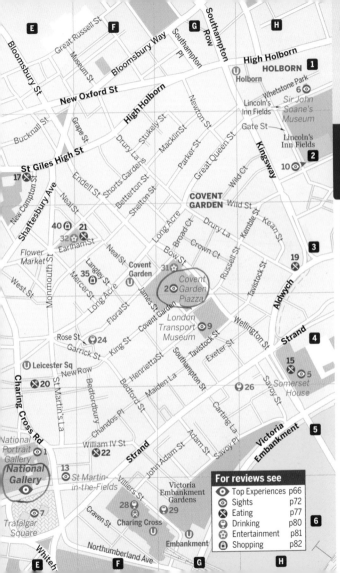

National Gallery & Covent Garden

E
Bloomsbury St
Great Russell St
Museum St
F
Bloomsbury Way
Southampton Pl
Southampton Row
G
Southampton Row
H

High Holborn **1**
HOLBORN
U Holborn
Whetstone Park
6
Lincoln's Inn Fields
Sir John Soane's Museum
Gate St
Lincoln's Inn Fields
10
2

New Oxford St
High Holborn
Bucknall St
Grape St
Drury La
Stukely St
Macklin St
Parker St
Newton St
Great Queen St
Kingsway
Wild Ct

St Giles High St
17
New Compton St
Shaftesbury Ave
Endell St
Shorts Gardens
Betterton St
Shelton St
COVENT GARDEN
Wild St
Kemble St
Kean St

Neal St
40 **21**
32
Earlham St
Long Acre
Broad Ct
Drury La
Crown Ct
Russell St
Tavistock St
Aldwych
19
3

Flower Market
West St
Monmouth St
Neal St
Langley St
Mercer St
Long Acre
Covent Garden **U**
Floral St
James St
35
31
Bow St
Covent Garden Piazza
2
London Transport Museum
9
Wellington St
Strand
4

Rose St
24
Garrick St
King St
Covent Garden
Southampton St
Tavistock St
Exeter St
Savoy St
15
5
Somerset House

U Leicester Sq
New Row
Henrietta St
Bedford St
Maiden La
Carting La
26

Charing Cross Rd
20
St Martin's La
Chandos Pl
Bedfordbury
Adam St
Savoy Pl
Victoria Embankment
5

National Portrait Gallery
1
William IV St
13
St Martin-in-the-Fields
22
Strand
John Adam St

National Gallery
Villiers St
Victoria Embankment Gardens
28
29
Charing Cross
Craven St
7
Trafalgar Square

U Embankment
Northumberland Ave

Whiteh...
E
F
G
H
6

For reviews see	
◉ Top Experiences	p66
◎ Sights	p72
✕ Eating	p77
🍷 Drinking	p80
★ Entertainment	p81
🛍 Shopping	p82

Sights

National Portrait Gallery

GALLERY

1 ◎ MAP P70, E5

What makes the National Portrait Gallery so compelling is its familiarity; in many cases, you will have heard of the subject (royals, scientists, politicians, celebrities) or the artist (Andy Warhol, Annie Leibovitz, Lucian Freud), but you won't necessarily recognise the face. The collection is organised chronologically, and then by theme. At time of research the gallery was closed till spring 2023 for renovations. (📞020-7306 0055; www.npg.org.uk; St Martin's Pl; admission free; ⊗10am-6pm Sat-Thu, to 9pm Fri; Ⓤ Charing Cross or Leicester Sq)

Covent Garden Piazza

LANDMARK

2 ◎ MAP P70, G3

London's wholesale fruit-and-vegetable market until 1974 is now mostly the preserve of visitors, who flock here to shop among the quaint Italian-style arcades, eat and drink in the myriad cafes and restaurants, browse through eclectic market stalls in the Apple Market, toss coins at street performers on the West Piazza and traipse through the fun London Transport Museum (p75).

The open square in front of **St Paul's Church** (📞020-7836 5221; www.actorschurch.org; Bedford St; ⊗8.30am-5.30pm Mon-Fri, 9am-1pm Sun, hours vary Sat; Ⓤ Covent Garden) – nicknamed the Actors'

Covent Garden Piazza

Church – has long been a place of performance: even Samuel Pepys' diary from 1662 mentions an Italian puppet play with a character named Punch. The best views of the action today are from the upper terrace of the Punch & Judy pub.

An old painted noticeboard with rules and charges for vendors can still be found lurking in one of the alleys on the northern side, and black-and-white photos of Covent Garden's days as a food traders' market line the walls of the narrow passages.

The kitsch is hauled out for the quirky Rent Ceremony, in which the chairman and trustees strut around the piazza, accompanied by a live band, to pay Covent Garden's landlord the yearly rent of five red apples and five posies of flowers. It usually takes place in June. (020-7420 5856; www.covent garden.london; U Covent Garden)

Chinatown Gate   LANDMARK

3 MAP P70, D4

Northwest of Leicester Sq but a world away in atmosphere, this grand red-pillared and tile-roofed gate marks the entrance into Chinatown. Although not as big as Chinatowns in other world-class cities – it's just Lisle and Gerrard Sts, really – London's version is a lively quarter with street signs in Chinese script, red lanterns strung up across the streets bobbing in the breeze, and noodle shops, restaurants and Asian supermarkets crammed in cheek by jowl.

The quality of food varies enormously, but there's a good choice of places for dim sum and other cuisines from across China and other parts of Asia.

To see the area at its effervescent best, time your visit for Lunar New Year in late January or early February. London's original Chinatown was at Limehouse in the East End, but moved here after heavy bombardments in WWII. (www.chinatown.co.uk; Wardour St; U Leicester Sq)

Soho   AREA

4 MAP P70, D3

In a district that was once pastureland, the name Soho is thought to have evolved from a hunting cry. While the centre of London nightlife has shifted east, and Soho has recently seen landmark clubs and music venues shut down, the neighbourhood definitely comes into its own in the evenings and remains a proud gay district. You'll be charmed by the area's vitality during the day, too.

At Soho's northern end, leafy Soho Sq is the area's back garden. It was laid out in 1681 and originally called King's Sq; a statue of Charles II stands in its northern half. In the centre is a tiny half-timbered mock-Tudor cottage built as a gardener's shed in the 1870s. The space below it was used as an underground bomb shelter during WWII.

South of the square is Dean St, lined with restaurants and bars.

No 28 was the home of Karl Marx and his family from 1851 to 1856; they lived here in extreme poverty as Marx researched and wrote *Das Kapital*.

Old Compton St is the epicentre of Soho's gay village. It's a street loved by all, gay or other, for its great bars, risqué shops and general good vibes.

Seducer and heart-breaker Casanova and opium-addicted writer Thomas de Quincey lived on nearby Greek St, while the parallel Frith St housed Mozart at No 20 for a year from 1764. (U Tottenham Court Rd or Leicester Sq)

Somerset House

HISTORIC BUILDING

5 ◎ MAP P70, H4

Designed in 1775 for government departments and royal societies – perhaps the world's first office block – Somerset House now contains galleries, restaurants and cafes that encircle a lovely open courtyard and extend to an elevated sun-trap terrace. The Embankment Galleries are devoted to temporary exhibitions (usually related to photography, design or fashion). In summer, the grand courtyard hosts open-air live performances, dancing fountains for kids to cool off in and the **Film4 Summer Screen** (📞 0333 320 2836; tickets from £19; ⏱ Aug), plus an atmospheric ice-skating rink in winter. (📞 020-7845 4600; www.somersethouse.org.uk; The Strand; ⏱ courtyard 7.30am-11pm; U Temple)

Sir John Soane's Museum

MUSEUM

6 ◎ MAP P70, H1

This museum is one of the most atmospheric and fascinating in London. The Georgian building was the beautiful, bewitching home of architect Sir John Soane (1753–1837), which he bequeathed to the nation through an Act of Parliament on condition that it remain untouched after his death and free to visit. It's brimming with Soane's vast collection of art and archaeological purchases, as well as intriguing personal effects and curiosities. The house-museum represents his exquisite and eccentric tastes and proclivities. (📞 020-7405 2107; www.soane.org; 13 Lincoln's Inn Fields; admission free; ⏱ 10am-5pm Wed-Sun; U Holborn)

Trafalgar Square

SQUARE

7 ◎ MAP P70, E6

Opened to the public in 1844, Trafalgar Sq is the true centre of London, where rallies and marches take place, tens of thousands of revellers usher in the New Year and locals congregate for anything from communal open-air cinema and Christmas celebrations to political protests. It is dominated by the 52m-high Nelson's Column, guarded by four bronze lion statues, and ringed by many splendid buildings, including the National Gallery (p66) and the church of St Martin-in-the-Fields (p77). (U Charing Cross or Embankment)

Fourth Plinth Project

Three of the four plinths at the corners of Trafalgar Sq are occupied by notables: King George IV on horseback, and military men General Sir Charles Napier and Major General Sir Henry Havelock. The fourth, originally intended for a statue of William IV, remained largely vacant for more than a century and a half. The Royal Society of Arts conceived what is now called the Fourth Plinth Commission in 1999, deciding to use the empty space for works by contemporary artists. Works exhibited for 18 months in 'the smallest sculpture park in the world' are invariably both fun and challenging, creating a sense of dissonance with the grand surrounds of Trafalgar Sq.

St James's Piccadilly CHURCH

8 ⊙ MAP P70, B6

The only church (1684) Christopher Wren built from scratch and one of a handful established on a new site (most of the other London churches are replacements for those destroyed in the Great Fire), this simple building substitutes what some might call the pompous flourishes of Wren's most famous churches with a warm and elegant accessibility. The baptismal font portraying Adam and Eve on the shaft and the altar reredos are by Grinling Gibbons. (☏020-7734 4511; www. sjp.org.uk; 197 Piccadilly; ⊙8am-8pm; U Piccadilly Circus)

London Transport Museum MUSEUM

9 ⊙ MAP P70, G4

Housed in Covent Garden's former flower-market building, this captivating museum looks at how London developed as a result of

better transport. It's stuffed full of horse-drawn omnibuses, vintage Underground carriages and old double-decker buses (some of which you can clamber through, making this something of a kids' playground). The gift shop also sells great London souvenirs such as retro Tube posters and pillows made from the same fabric as the train seats. (☏020-7379 6344; www. ltmuseum.co.uk; Covent Garden Piazza; adult/child £18/free; ⊙10am-6pm; ♦; U Covent Garden)

Lincoln's Inn HISTORIC BUILDING

10 ⊙ MAP P70, H2

The attractive Lincoln's Inn has a chapel with lovely stained glass, a pleasant square, and picturesque gardens that invite a stroll, especially early or late in the day. The Great Hall, although closed to the public, is visible through the gates and is relatively intact, with original 15th-century buildings, including the Tudor Lincoln's Inn Gatehouse (33 Chancery Lane).

Piccadilly Circus

Inigo Jones helped plan the well-preserved chapel, which was built in 1623. (☎020-7405 1393; www.lincolnsinn.org.uk; Lincoln's Inn Fields, Serle St; ☼grounds 7am-7pm Mon-Fri, chapel 9am-5pm Mon-Fri; ⓤHolborn)

Piccadilly Circus SQUARE

11 ◉ MAP P70, C5

Architect John Nash had originally designed Regent St and Piccadilly in the 1820s to be the two most elegant streets in London but, restrained by city planners, he couldn't fully realise his dream. He may be disappointed, but suitably astonished, by Piccadilly Circus today: a traffic maelstrom, deluged by visitors and flanked by high-tech advertisements. (ⓤPiccadilly Circus)

All Saints Margaret Street CHURCH

12 ◉ MAP P70, A1

In 1859, architect William Butterfield completed one of the country's most supreme examples of High Victorian Gothic architecture, with extraordinary tiling and sumptuous stained glass. All Saints was selected by the head of English Heritage in 2014 as one of the top 10 buildings in the UK that have changed the face of the nation, a list that included Westminster Abbey and Christ Church in Oxford. (☎020-7636 1788; www.allsaintsmargaretstreet.org.uk; 7 Margaret St; ☼7am-7pm Mon, Tue, Thu & Fri, 8.30am-7pm Wed, 11am-7pm Sat; ⓤOxford Circus)

St Martin-in-the-Fields CHURCH

13 MAP P70, E5

This parish church to the Royal Family is a delightful fusion of neoclassical and baroque styles. It was designed by architect James Gibbs, completed in 1726 and served as a model for many wooden churches in New England, USA. The church is well known for its excellent classical music concerts (£9 to £32), many by candlelight, and its links to the Chinese community (with services in English, Mandarin and Cantonese). (☎020-7766 1100; www.stmartin-in-the-fields.org; Trafalgar Sq; ⏰8.30am-6pm Mon-Fri, 9am-6pm Sat & Sun; ☒Charing Cross)

Eating

Palomar ISRAELI ££

14 MAP P70, C4

Packed and praised from the day it opened, Palomar is a wonderful Israeli/Levantine restaurant with the look of a 1930s diner and the constant theatre of expert chefs whipping up magic behind the central zinc bar. Unusual dishes such as date-glazed octopus with harissa will blow you away, as will slow-cooked Tel Aviv seafood or beetroot labneh with parsley vinaigrette.

It's usually possible to get one or two of the 16 bar stools at shortish notice for lunch, but book further ahead for a table in the dining room, or for dinner. (☎020-7439 8777; www.thepalomar.co.uk; 34 Rupert St; mains £14-16; ⏰noon-2.30pm & 5.30-11pm Mon-Sat, 12.30-3.30pm & 6-9pm Sun; 📶; ☒Piccadilly Circus)

Spring BRITISH £££

15 MAP P70, H4

White walls, ball chandeliers and columns are offset by the odd blossom in this restored Victorian drawing room in Somerset House (p74). Award-winning Australian chef Skye Gyngell leads a team dedicated to sustainability – no single-use plastic and an early-evening scratch menu (£25 for three courses) using food that would otherwise be wasted. Desserts are legendary. (☎020-3011 0115; www.springrestaurant.co.uk; New Wing, Somerset House, Lancaster Pl; mains £29-33, 2-/3-course lunch £29/32; ⏰noon-2.30pm & 5.30-10.30pm Mon-Sat; ☒Temple)

Kiln THAI ££

16 MAP P70, B4

Crowned the UK's best restaurant in 2018, this tiny Thai grill cooks up a storm in its long, narrow kitchen, overseen by diners on their stools. The short menu rides the small-plates wave and works best with a few friends so you can taste a greater variety. The beef-neck curry is phenomenal, as are the claypot-baked glass noodles. (www.kilnsoho.com; 58 Brewer St; dishes £4.50-14; ⏰noon-3pm & 5-11pm Mon-Thu, noon-11pm Fri & Sat, to 10pm Sun; ☒Piccadilly Circus)

Kanada-Ya
RAMEN £

17 🗺 MAP P70, E2

In the debate over London's best ramen, we're still voting for this one. With no reservations taken, queues can get impressive outside this tiny and enormously popular canteen, where ramen cooked in *tonkotsu* (pork-bone broth) draws in diners from near and far. The noodles arrive at just the right temperature and hardness, steeped in a delectable broth and rich flavours. (📞020-7240 0232; www.kanada-ya.com; 64 St Giles High St; mains £11-13; 🕔noon-3pm & 5-10.30pm Mon-Sat, to 8.30pm Sun; Ⓤ Tottenham Court Rd)

Foyer & Reading Room at Claridge's
BRITISH £££

18 🗺 MAP P70, A3

Refreshing the better sort of West End shopper since 1856, the jaw-dropping Foyer and Reading Room at Claridge's, refulgent with art-deco mirrors and a Dale Chihuly glass sculpture, really is a memorable dining space. Refined food is served at all mealtimes, but many choose to nibble in best aristocratic fashion on the finger sandwiches and pastries of a classic afternoon tea. Note that smart attire is always required. (📞020-7107 8886; www.claridges.co.uk; Brook St; afternoon tea £70, with champagne £80-90; 🕔7am-11pm Mon-Sat, 8am-11pm Sun, afternoon tea 2.45-5.30pm; 📶; Ⓤ Bond St)

Delaunay
EUROPEAN ££

19 🗺 MAP P70, H3

This immaculate spot channels the majesty of the grand cafes of Central Europe. Schnitzels, sausages and fish take pride of place on the menu, which is rounded out with Alsatian *tarte flambée* (thin-crust 'pizzas' with crème fraiche, onions and bacon lardons) and a rotating *Tagesteller* (dish of the day). The more relaxed **Delaunay Counter** (soups & sandwiches £7.50-8.50; 🕔7am-8.30pm Mon-Fri, 10.30am-8.30pm Sat, 11am-5.30pm Sun) is next door. (📞020-7499 8558; www.thedelaunay.com; 55 Aldwych; mains £19-26; 🕔7am-11pm Mon-Fri, 8am-11pm Sat, 9am-10pm Sun; 📶; Ⓤ Temple or Covent Garden)

J Sheekey
SEAFOOD £££

20 🗺 MAP P70, E4

A jewel of the Covent Garden dining scene, this incredibly smart restaurant was opened by 1890s fishmonger Josef Sheekey on the permission of Lord Salisbury (who wanted somewhere to eat after the theatre). It has four elegant, discreet and spacious wood-panelled rooms in which to savour the riches of the sea, cooked simply but exquisitely. Set menus for two/three courses are £25/30. (📞020-7240 2565; www.j-sheekey. co.uk; 28-32 St Martin's Ct; mains £27-36; 🕔noon-3pm & 5pm-midnight Mon-Sat, noon-3.30pm & 5.30-10.30pm Sun; 📶; Ⓤ Leicester Sq)

Milhojas **dessert, Barrafina**

Seven Dials Market

STREET FOOD £

21  MAP P70, F3

In a former banana warehouse (thus the banana motif) and reminiscent of New York's famous Chelsea Market, this two-storey indoor street-food collective delivers everything from vegan tacos at Club Mexicana and Japanese soul food at the tiny outpost of Brixton's Nanban to choice cheese and wine pairings at Pick & Cheese. Sun streams through the glass skylights by day; live music gets the party vibe going at night. (www.sevendialsmarket.com; Earlham St; ⏱11am-11pm Mon-Sat, noon-10.30pm Sun; Ⓤ Covent Garden)

Barrafina

TAPAS ££

22  MAP P70, F5

With no reservations, you may need to get in line for an hour or so at this restaurant that produces some of the best tapas in town. Divine mouthfuls are served on each plate, from the prawns with roasted *piquillo* pepper to the Iberian pork ribs and chargrilled artichokes, so you may think it worth the wait. There's a maximum group size of four and a couple of tables on the pavement. (☏020-7440 1456; www.barrafina. co.uk; 10 Adelaide St; basic tapas £4-7, larger plates £9-17; ⏱noon-3pm & 5-11pm Mon-Sat; Ⓤ Embankment or Leicester Sq)

West End on the Cheap

London, the West End especially, can be an expensive destination, but there are plenty of ways to make your pennies last. Many of the top museums are free, so give them priority over the more commercial attractions. The West End is compact, so choose to walk, take the bus (it's cheaper than the Tube) or hire a **Santander Cycle** (☏ 0343 222 6666; www.tfl.gov. uk/modes/cycling/santander-cycles) for the day. Finally, go out early – bars in the West End often have a 'happy hour' with cheaper drinks.

Drinking

Artesian   COCKTAIL BAR

23 🚇 MAP P70, A1

For a dose of colonial glamour with a touch of Oriental elegance, the sumptuous bar at the Langham hits many marks. Its cocktails (from £20) have won multiple awards, and the bar itself has been acclaimed the world's best. Its name acknowledges the 360ft-deep well beneath the hotel and, metaphorically, the 'source of indulgence' to be found within. (☏ 020-7636 1000; www.artesian-bar. co.uk; Langham Hotel, 1c Portland Pl; ⊙ 11am-1am Mon-Wed, to 2am Thu-Sat, to midnight Sun; 🛜; 🚇 Oxford Circus)

Lamb & Flag   PUB

24 🚇 MAP P70, F4

Perpetually busy, the pint-sized Lamb & Flag is full of charm and history: there's been a public house here since at least 1772, when it was known as the Cooper's Arms and infamous for staging bare-knuckle boxing matches. Rain or shine, you'll have to elbow your way through the merry crowd drinking outside to get to the bar. (☏ 020-7497 9504; www.lamband flagcoventgarden.co.uk; 33 Rose St; ⊙ 11am-11pm Mon-Sat, noon-10.30pm Sun; 🚇 Covent Garden)

Magritte Bar   COCKTAIL BAR

25 🚇 MAP P70, A2

Sip a bourbon or a classic cocktail in the 1920s art-deco ambience of this stylish bar at the hallmark Beaumont hotel. It's central, glam and like a private members' club, but far from stuffy. Only a few years old, the Margritte Bar feels like it's been pouring drinks since the days of the flapper and the jazz age. (☏ 020-7499 1001; www. thebeaumont.com/dining/american-bar; Beaumont, Brown Hart Gardens; ⊙ 11.30am-midnight Mon-Sat, to 11pm Sun; 🛜; 🚇 Bond St)

American Bar   COCKTAIL BAR

26 🚇 MAP P70, H5

Home of the Lonely Street, Concrete Jungle and other house cocktails named after iconic songs collected in the 'Savoy Songbook', the seriously dishy American Bar s a London icon, with soft blue furniture, gleaming art-deco lines and live piano jazz from 6.30pm nightly. Cocktails start at £20 and peak at a stupefying £5000 (for the Sazerac, containing cognac from 1858). (☑020-7836 4343; www. fairmont.com/savoy-london/dining/ americanbar; The Savoy Hotel, Strand; ⊙11.30am-midnight Mon-Sat, noon-midnight Sun; ☑; Ⓤ Temple, Charing Cross or Embankment)

French House PUB

27 🚇 MAP P70, D4

This legendary, twin-storied bohemian boozer has quite a history: it was the meeting place of the Free French Forces during WWII and de Gaulle is said to have drunk here often, while Dylan Thomas, Peter O'Toole and Francis Bacon all measured their length on the wooden floor at least once. Expect to share space with media and theatre types enjoying liquid lunches. (☑020-7437 2477; www. frenchhousesoho.com; 49 Dean St; ⊙noon-11pm Mon-Sat, to 10.30pm Sun; Ⓤ Leicester Sq)

Heaven GAY

28 🚇 MAP P70, F6

Encouraging hedonism since 1979, when it opened on the site of a former roller disco, this perennially popular mixed/gay bar under the Charing Cross arches hosts excellent gigs and club nights, and has hosted New Order, The Birthday Party, Killing Joke and many a legendary act. Monday's mixed party Popcorn offers one of the best weeknight's clubbing in the capital.

The celebrated G-A-Y takes place here on Thursday (G-A-Y Porn Idol), Friday (G-A-Y Camp Attack) and Saturday (plain ol' G-A-Y). (☑020-7930 2020; www. heavennightclub-london.com; Villiers St; ⊙11pm-5am Mon, to 4am Thu & Fri, 10.30pm-5am Sat; Ⓤ Embankment or Charing Cross)

Gordon's Wine Bar WINE BAR

29 🚇 MAP P70, G6

Quite possibly the oldest wine bar in London (it opened in 1890), cavernous, candlelit and atmospheric Gordon's is a victim of its own success – it's relentlessly busy, and unless you arrive before the office crowd does, forget about landing a table. Nibble on cheese, bread and olives with your plonk – there's even a vegan/organic wine list. (☑020-7930 1408; www.gordonswinebar.com; 47 Villiers St; ⊙11am-11pm Mon-Sat, noon-10pm Sun; Ⓤ Embankment or Charing Cross)

Entertainment

Wigmore Hall CLASSICAL MUSIC

30 ⭐ MAP P70, A1

Wigmore Hall, built in 1901 as a piano showroom, is one of the best and most active classical-music venues in town, with more than 460 concerts a year. This isn't just because of its fantastic acoustics and great variety of concerts, but also because of the sheer quality

West End Budget Flicks

Leicester Sq cinema-ticket prices are very high, so wait until the first-runs have moved to the **Prince Charles Cinema** (Map p70, D4; [☎] 020-7494 3654; www.princecharlescinema.com; 7 Leicester Pl; [U] Leicester Sq), central London's cheapest cinema, where non-members pay only £9 to £11.50 for new releases. Also on the cards are mini-festivals, Q&As with film directors, classics, sleepover movie marathons and exuberant singalong screenings of films such as *Frozen*, *The Sound of Music* and *Rocky Horror Picture Show* (£16).

of the performances. ([☎] 020-7935 2141; www.wigmore-hall.org.uk; 36 Wigmore St; [U] Bond St)

Royal Opera House OPERA

31 ⭐ MAP P70, G3

Opera and ballet have a fantastic setting on Covent Garden Piazza, and a night here is a sumptuous affair. Although the programme has modern influences, the main attractions are still the classic productions with their world-class performers. A £50-million revamp finished in October 2018, with new areas open to the non-ticketed public for the first time, including the cafe and bar. ([☎] 020-7304 4000; www.roh.org.uk; Bow St; ⊙ gift shop & cafe from 10am; [U] Covent Garden)

Donmar Warehouse THEATRE

32 ⭐ MAP P70, E3

The 250-seat Donmar Warehouse is London's 'thinking person's theatre'. With new artistic director Michael Longhurst, works in progress are more provocative and less celebrity-driven than traditional West End theatre. The 2020 programme included works from playwrights such as Nina Segal and Caryl Churchill. ([☎] 020-3282 3808; www.donmarwarehouse.com; 41 Earlham St; [U] Covent Garden)

Ronnie Scott's JAZZ

33 ⭐ MAP P70, D3

Ronnie Scott's jazz club opened in 1959 and became widely known as Britain's best, hosting such luminaries as Miles Davis, Charlie Parker, Ella Fitzgerald, Sarah Vaughan and Count Basie. The club continues to build upon its formidable reputation by presenting a range of big names and new talent. Book in advance, or come for a more informal gig at Upstairs @ Ronnie's. ([☎] 020-7439 0747; www.ronniescotts.co.uk; 47 Frith St; ⊙ 6pm-3am Mon-Sat, noon-4pm & 6.30pm-midnight Sun; [U] Leicester Sq or Tottenham Court Rd)

Shopping

Foyles BOOKS

34 🔒 MAP P70, D3

London's most legendary bookshop, where you can find even the most obscure titles. Once synonymous with chaos, Foyles got its

Royal Opera House

act together and now this carefully designed store is a joy to explore. The cafe is on the 5th floor, plus a small gallery for art exhibitions. Grant & Cutler, the UK's largest foreign-language bookseller, is on the 4th floor. (📞020-7434 1574; www.foyles.co.uk; 107 Charing Cross Rd; ⏰9.30am-9pm Mon-Sat, noon-6pm Sun; Ⓤ Tottenham Court Rd)

Stanfords

BOOKS

35 🔒 MAP P70, F3

Trading since 1853, this grandaddy of travel bookshops and seasoned seller of maps, guides and globes is a destination in its own right. Polar explorer Ernest Shackleton, Victorian missionary David Livingstone and writer and presenter Michael Palin have all shopped here. In 2019 Stanfords

left the iconic Long Acre building it had been housed in since 1901 and moved around the corner to its new address. (📞020-7836 1321; www.stanfords.co.uk; 7 Mercer Walk; ⏰9am-8pm Mon-Sat, noon-6pm Sun; Ⓤ Leicester Sq or Covent Garden)

Liberty

DEPARTMENT STORE

36 🔒 MAP P70, A3

One of London's most recognisable shops, Liberty department store has a white-and-wood-beam Tudor Revival facade that lures shoppers in to browse luxury contemporary fashion, homewares, cosmetics and accessories, all at sky-high prices. Liberty is known for its fabrics and has a full haberdashery department; a classic London gift or souvenir is a Liberty fabric print, especially in the form

of a scarf. (☎020-7734 1234; www.
libertylondon.com; Regent St, entrance
on Great Marlborough St; ⌚10am-
8pm Mon-Sat, 11.30am-6pm Sun; 📶;
Ⓤ Oxford Circus)

Hamleys
TOYS

37 🔒 MAP P70, A4

The biggest and oldest toy emporium in the world, Hamleys houses
six floors of fun for kids of all ages,
from the basement's Star Wars and
Harry Potter collections up to Lego
World, a sweet shop, and a tiny cafe
on the 5th floor. Staff on each level
have opened the packaging and
are playing with everything from
boomerangs to bubbles. Kids will
happily spend hours here planning
their Santa letters. (☎0371 704
1977; www.hamleys.com; 188-196

Regent St; ⌚10am-9pm Mon-Fri,
9.30am-9pm Sat, noon-6pm Sun; 🚻;
Ⓤ Oxford Circus)

Vivienne Westwood
FASHION & ACCESSORIES

38 🔒 MAP P70, A4

The fashion doyenne of the punk
and new-wave aesthetic, West-
wood has always had a reputation for being controversial and
political. She continues to design
collections as bold, innovative
and provocative as ever, featuring
19th-century-inspired bustiers,
wedge shoes, tartan and sharp
tailoring. (☎020-7439 1109; www.
viviennewestwood.com; 44 Conduit St;
⌚10am-6pm Mon-Wed, Fri & Sat, to
7pm Thu, noon-5pm Sun; Ⓤ Bond St or
Oxford Circus)

Neal's Yard Dairy

Regent Street

The handsome border dividing bar-hoppers of Soho from the Gucci-heeled hedge-fund managers of Mayfair, Regent St was designed by John Nash as a ceremonial route linking Carlton House, the Prince Regent's long-demolished town residence, with the 'wilds' of Regent's Park. Nash had to downsize his plan and build the thoroughfare on a curve, but Regent St is today a well-subscribed shopping street lined with some lovely listed buildings.

Its anchor tenant is undoubtedly Hamleys, London's premier toy and game store. Regent St is also famous for its Christmas light displays, which get switched on with some fanfare (usually around mid-November).

Sounds of the Universe
MUSIC

39 MAP P70, C3

Outlet of the Soul Jazz Records label: explorers of wild, wonderful and often forgotten corners of black music who bring back gems for their legendary compilations. Vinyl fetishists will love the many brilliant, previously rare reissues on sale. (020-7734 3430; www.soundsoftheuniverse.com; 7 Broadwick St; 10am-7.30pm Sat, 11.30am-5.30pm Sun; Oxford Circus, Tottenham Court Rd)

Neal's Yard Dairy
FOOD

40 MAP P70, E3

A fabulous, fragrant cheese house that would fit in somewhere in rural England, this place is proof that Britain can produce top-quality cheeses in most classes. There are more than 70 varieties of English and Irish cheeses that the shopkeepers will let you taste, including independent farmhouse brands. Condiments, pickles, jams and chutneys are also on sale. (020-7240 5700; www.nealsyarddairy.co.uk; 17 Shorts Gardens; 10am-7pm Mon-Sat; Covent Garden)

Explore ⊕

British Museum & Bloomsbury

Bookish Bloomsbury puts a leisurely and genteel spin on central London. Home to the British Museum, the British Library, universities, publishing houses, literary pubs and gorgeous Georgian squares, Bloomsbury is deeply but accessibly cultured. You could spend all day in the British Museum, but there's a tantalising choice of options outside, with excellent pubs and restaurants nearby.

The Short List

o *British Museum (p88)* Admiring ancient civilisations going back seven millennia.

o *British Library (p96)* Learning about the treasures of the English language.

o *Wellcome Collection (p96)* Exploring a unique museum where science and art meet.

o *Coal Drops Yard (p97)* Strolling the newly redeveloped industrial heartland by Kings Cross.

o *London Review Bookshop (p104)* Browsing a wide range of titles at this excellent bookshop.

Getting There & Around

U Get off at Tottenham Court Rd (Northern and Central Lines), Goodge St (Northern Line), Russell Sq (Piccadilly Line) or Euston Sq (Circle, Hammersmith & City and Metropolitan Lines).

🚌 For the British Museum and Russell Sq, take bus 98 along Oxford St; bus 91 runs from Whitehall/Trafalgar Sq to the British Library.

Neighbourhood Map on p94

Bedford Sq (p93) WILLY BARTON/SHUTTERSTOCK ©

Top Experience 📷

Wander Through Time at the British Museum

Britain's most visited attraction for a decade, the British Museum draws in 5.8 million visitors each year. It's an exhaustive and exhilarating stampede through world cultures over millennia, with 90 galleries of over 80,000 exhibits devoted to ancient civilisations, from Egypt to western Asia, the Middle East, Rome and Greece, India, Africa, and prehistoric and Roman Britain.

◎ MAP P94, C7

✆ 020-7323 8000

www.britishmuseum.org

Great Russell St

admission free

🕑 10am-5.30pm Sat-Thu, to 8.30pm Fri

Ⓤ Tottenham Court Rd or Russell Sq

History of the Museum

The museum was founded in 1753 when royal physician Hans Sloane sold his 'cabinet of curiosities' for the then-princely sum of £20,000, raised by national lottery. The collection opened to the public for free in 1759, and the museum has since kept expanding through judicious acquisitions, bequests and controversial imperial plundering.

The Great Court

The first thing you'll see on entry is the Great Court covered with a spectacular glass-and-steel roof designed by Norman Foster in 2000. It is the largest covered public square in Europe. In its centre is the celebrated Reading Room, currently closed, which has been frequented by the big brains of history, from Mahatma Gandhi to Karl Marx.

Enlightenment Galleries

Formerly known as the King's Library, this stunning neoclassical space (room 1) just off the Great Court was built between 1823 and 1827 and was the first part of the new museum building as it is seen today. Through fascinating artefacts, the collection traces how such disciplines as biology, archaeology, linguistics and geography emerged during the Enlightenment of the 18th century.

Ancient Egypt

The star of the show is the Ancient Egypt collection upstairs. It comprises sculptures, fine jewellery, papyrus texts, coffins and mummies, including the beautiful and intriguing Mummy of Katebet (room 63). The most prized item in the museum is the Rosetta Stone (room 4), the key to deciphering Egyptian hieroglyphics. Nearby is the enormous bust of the pharaoh Ramesses II (room 4).

★ **Top Tips**

○ The museum has two entrances: one on Great Russell St and the other on Montague Pl (usually less busy).

○ Don't attempt to see all sections of the museum; there are more than 5km of corridors. Choose one or two periods or civilisations (eg Ancient Egypt, Roman Britain, Japan and Korea).

✕ **Take a Break**

The British Museum is vast so you'll need to recharge. **Abeno** (www.abeno.co.uk; 47 Museum St; mains £13-21; ◷noon-10pm; Ⓤ Holborn) is nearby for savoury pancakes and other dishes from Japan.

For something more traditional, enjoy a cream tea at **Tea & Tattle** (www.teaandtattle.com; 41 Great Russell St; afternoon tea for one/two £19/38; ◷9am-6pm Mon-Fri, noon-4pm Sat; ☏; Ⓤ Tottenham Court Rd) just across the road.

Conquering the Museum

The museum is huge, so make a few focused visits if you have time, and consider taking one of the free tours. There are free 30-minute Eye-opener tours of individual galleries, lunchtime gallery talks, and an Around the World in 90 Minutes tour (£14, limited capacity). Audio and family guides (adult/child £7/6) in 10 languages are available from the desk in the Great Court. For activity packs for children (by age) which will make their visit much more engaging, head to the Families Desk in the Great Hall.

Assyrian Treasures

Assyrian treasures from ancient Mesopotamia include the winged bulls from Khorsabad (room 10), at 16 tonnes the heaviest object in the museum. Behind it are the exquisite lion hunt reliefs from Ninevah (room 10) dating from the 7th century BCE, which influenced Greek sculpture. Such antiquities are all the more significant after the so-called Islamic State's bulldozing of Nimrud in 2015.

Parthenon Sculptures

A major highlight of the museum is the Parthenon sculptures (room 18). The 80m-long marble frieze is thought to be of the Great Panathenaea, a festival in honour of the Greek goddess Athena held every four years.

Mildenhall Treasure & Lindow Man

Upstairs are finds from Britain and the rest of Europe (rooms 40 to 51). Many go back to Roman times, when the empire spread across much of the continent, including the Mildenhall Treasure (room 49), a collection of almost three dozen pieces of 4th-century-CE Roman silverware unearthed in Suffolk with both pagan and early Christian motifs. Lindow Man (room 50) is the well-preserved remains of a 1st-century man discovered in a bog near Manchester in northern England in 1984.

Sutton Hoo Ship Burial

The medieval artefacts from the Sutton Hoo Ship Burial (room 41), an elaborate Anglo-Saxon burial site from Suffolk dating back to the 7th century, are another unmissable highlight of the museum.

Lewis Chessmen

Perennial favourites are the lovely Lewis Chessmen (room 40), some of the 82 12th-century game pieces carved from walrus tusk and whale teeth that were found on a remote Scottish island in the early 19th century.

Museum Extension

The British Museum's long-awaited extension, the £135 million World Conservation & Exhibitions Centre, opened in 2014, in the same year as the Sainsbury Exhibitions Gallery, which hosts high-profile exhibitions.

British Museum

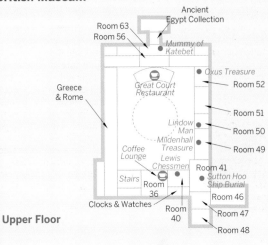

Upper Floor

Room 63
Room 56
Ancient Egypt Collection
Mummy of Katebet
Oxus Treasure
Room 52
Great Court Restaurant
Room 51
Lindow Man
Room 50
Mildenhall Treasure
Room 49
Greece & Rome
Coffee Lounge
Lewis Chessmen
Room 41
Sutton Hoo Ship Burial
Stairs
Room 46
Room 36
Room 47
Clocks & Watches
Room 40
Room 48

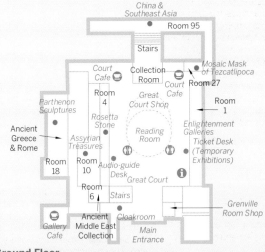

Ground Floor

China & Southeast Asia
Room 95
Stairs
Court Cafe
Collection Room
Court Cafe
Mosaic Mask of Tezcatlipoca
Room 27
Room 4
Great Court Shop
Room 1
Parthenon Sculptures
Rosetta Stone
Reading Room
Enlightenment Galleries
Ancient Greece & Rome
Assyrian Treasures
Ticket Desk (Temporary Exhibitions)
Room 18
Room 10
Audio-guide Desk
Room 6
Stairs
Great Court
Grenville Room Shop
Gallery Cafe
Ancient Middle East Collection
Cloakroom
Main Entrance
Great Russell St

Walking Tour 🚶

A Literary Walk Around Bloomsbury

Bloomsbury is indelibly associated with the literary circles that made this part of London their home. Charles Dickens, JM Barrie, WB Yeats, Virginia Woolf, TS Eliot, Sylvia Plath and other bold-faced names of English literature have all been associated with properties delightfully dotted around Bloomsbury and its attractive squares.

Walk Facts

Start Bedford Sq; U Goodge St

End Museum Tavern; U Holborn or Tottenham Court Rd

Length 1.1 miles; two to three hours

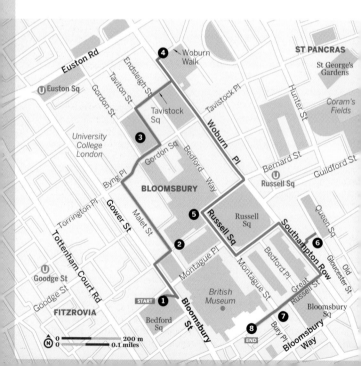

❶ Bedford Square

An eye-catching symbiosis of Bloomsbury's creative heritage and architectural charms, Bedford Sq is London's best-preserved Georgian square. The main office of Bloomsbury Publishing is at No 50. Sir Anthony Hope Hawkins, author of *The Prisoner of Zenda,* lived at No 41 while the Pre-Raphaelite Brotherhood was founded around the corner at 7 Gower St in 1848.

❷ Senate House

Along student-thronged Malet St, the splendid but intimidating art deco Senate House served as the Ministry of Information in WWII, inspiring George Orwell's Ministry of Truth in his novel *Nineteen Eighty-Four.* Orwell's wife, Eileen, worked in the censorship department between 1939 and 1942.

❸ Gordon Square

Once a private square, Gordon Sq is open to the public and a lovely place for a rest. Locals sit on benches reading, chatting and eating sandwiches when the sun shines. Blue plaques attest to the presence of literary greats.

❹ Woburn Walk

Irish poet and playwright WB Yeats lived at 5 Woburn Walk, a genteel lane just south of the church of St Pancras. A leading figure of the Celtic Revival and author of *The Tower,* WB Yeats was born in Dublin, but spent many years in London.

❺ Faber & Faber

The former offices of Faber & Faber are at the northwest corner of Russell Sq, marked with a blue plaque about TS Eliot, the American poet and playwright and first editor at Faber. The gardens and fountain at the centre of Russell Sq are great for recuperation, preferably on a bench under the trees.

❻ St George the Martyr

The 18th-century church of St George the Martyr, across from the historic Queen's Larder (p102) pub at the south end of Queen Sq, was where Ted Hughes and Sylvia Plath were married on 16 June 1956 (aka Bloomsday). They chose this date in honour of James Joyce.

❼ London Review Bookshop

It wouldn't be Bloomsbury without a good bookshop and the London Review Bookshop (p104) is one of London's finest. Affiliated with the London Review of Books, it has an eclectic selection of books and DVDs. Bookworms spend hours browsing the shelves or absorbed in new purchases in the shop's cafe.

❽ Museum Tavern

Karl Marx used to down a well-earned pint at the Museum Tavern (p102) after a hard day inventing communism in the British Museum Reading Room. The lovely pub set around a long bar is popular with academics, students, regulars and tourists alike.

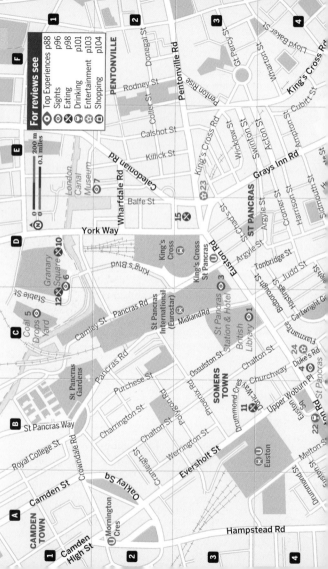

PENTONVILLE

For reviews see

	Top Experiences	p88
⊙	Sights	p96
⊗	Eating	p98
⊗	Drinking	p101
⊗	Entertainment	p103
⊟	Shopping	p104

ST PANCRAS

SOMERS TOWN

CAMDEN TOWN

Rosebery Ave

Phoenix Pl

Gough St

Calthorpe

Wren

Grays Inn Rd

John St

Roger St

Millman St

Doughty St

Charles Dickens Museum 8

Gray's Inn Gardens

Jockey's Fields

Bedford Row

Red Lion St

Northington St

Lamb's Conduit

Harpur St

Theobald's Rd

Chancery La

Serle St

Portugal St

Carey St

High Holborn

Lincoln's Inn Fields

Holborn 13

Procter St

Eagle St

Kingsway

Great Queen St

Parker St

Drury La

Coram's Fields

21

Brunswick Sq

Handel St

Bernard St

Marchmont St

Herbrand St

Woburn Pl

Guildford St

Great Ormond St

Boswell St

Queen Sq

Old Gloucester St

18

Southampton Row

Bedford Pl

Russell St

Russell Sq

Montague St

Bedford Way

Russell Sq

Bloomsbury Way

Bloomsbury Sq

Bury Pl

Great Russell St

25

19 Museum

20

Shaftesbury Ave

Grape St

Macklin St

Tavistock Sq

Gordon Sq

Carlton St

Gordon St

Woburn Pl

BLOOMSBURY

British Museum

Bloomsbury St

Bedford Sq

Malet St

Montague Pl

Bedford Ave

Morwell St

New Oxford St

29

St Giles High St

Buckn...

St Giles-in-the-Fields

27

Tottenham Court Rd

Soho Sq

Euston Sq

Wellcome Collection

University College London

Gower St

Store St

Ridgmount St

Chenies St

Alfred Pl

Tottenham Court Rd

Charlotte St

Gresse St

Rathbone Pl

Hanway St

Euston Rd

Warren St

Grafton Way

University St

Huntley St

Torrington Pl

Whitfield St

Goodge St

Goodge

Goodge St

Percy St

Rathbone St

Newman St

Berners Mews

Berners St

Charlotte St

17

Fitzroy St

Maple St

Howland St

Cleveland St

26

16

Great Titchfield St

Riding Wells St

Eastcastle St

Oxford St

9

Sights

British Library

LIBRARY

1 MAP P94, C3

Consisting of low-slung red-brick terraces and fronted by a large piazza with an oversized statue of Sir Isaac Newton, Colin St John Wilson's British Library building is an architectural wonder. Completed in 1998, it's home to some of the greatest treasures of the written word, including the *Codex Sinaiticus* (the first complete text of the New Testament), Leonardo da Vinci's notebooks and two copies of the Magna Carta (1215). (☎0330-333 1144; www.bl.uk; 96 Euston Rd; admission free; ◷9.30am-8pm Mon-Thu, to 6pm Fri, to 5pm Sat, 11am-5pm Sun; Ⓤ King's Cross St Pancras)

Wellcome Collection

MUSEUM

2 MAP P94, B5

Focusing on the interface of art, science and medicine, this clever and resourceful museum is fascinating. The museum's heart is Sir Henry Wellcome's collection of medical curiosities (saws for amputation, forceps through the ages, sex aids and amulets etc) in the Medicine Man gallery, which illustrate the universal fascination with health and the body across civilisations. In the Being Human gallery, interactive displays and provocative artworks are designed to make you ponder the human body and new forms of medical knowledge. (☎020-7611 2222; www.wellcomecollection. org; 183 Euston Rd; admission free;

British Library

⊘10am-6pm Tue, Wed & Fri-Sun, to 9pm Thu; Ⓤ Euston Sq or Euston)

St Pancras Station & Hotel · HISTORIC BUILDING

3 ◎ MAP P94, D3

Looking at the jaw-dropping Gothic splendour of St Pancras (1868), it's hard to believe that the Midland Grand Hotel languished empty for decades and even faced demolition in the 1960s. Now home to a five-star hotel, 67 luxury apartments and the Eurostar terminal, the entire complex has regained its former glory. Tours (£24; 10.30am, noon, 2pm and 3.30pm Saturday and Sunday) take you on a fascinating journey through the building's history, from its inception as the southern terminus for the Midland Railway line. (📞020-7843 7688; www.stpancras.com; Euston Rd; Ⓤ King's Cross St Pancras)

St Pancras Church · CHURCH

4 ◎ MAP P94, C4

This striking Greek Revival church has a tower designed to imitate the Temple of the Winds in Athens, a portico with six Ionic columns and a wing decorated with caryatids like the Erechtheion on the Acropolis. When it was completed in 1822 this was the most expensive new church to have been built in London since St Paul's Cathedral. Head to the atmospheric Crypt Gallery to see the latest art exhibition or drop in to a free lunchtime recital on a Thursday (1.15pm). (📞020-7388 1461; www.stpancraschurch.org; cnr

Surf & Rest

Although the books are all securely hidden away in the member's-only reading rooms, the British Library is a tranquil spot to rest and revive. There's free wifi throughout the building, excellent cafes and restaurant, plus special exhibitions to see.

Euston Rd & Upper Woburn Pl; ⊘8am-6pm Mon-Fri, 7.30-11.30am & 5.30-7pm Sun; Ⓤ Euston)

Coal Drops Yard · AREA

5 ◎ MAP P94, C1

The latest part of post-industrial King's Cross to be regenerated is this double-level shopping and eating arcade, curving its way along the Regent's Canal, just west of Granary Sq. Beautifully restored buildings from the 1850s used to transfer coal from rail wagons to road carts (and, later, '80s raves) are now home to independent clothing outlets, a range of restaurants and bars, and changing art installations. (www.coaldropsyard. com; Bagley Walk; ⊘varies by business; Ⓤ King's Cross St Pancras)

Granary Square · SQUARE

6 ◎ MAP P94, D1

Positioned on a sharp bend in the Regent's Canal north of King's Cross Station, Granary Sq is at the heart of a major redevelopment

British Museum & Bloomsbury Sights

of a 27-hectare expanse, once full of abandoned freight warehouses and an enormous granary. The square's most striking feature is the fountain made of 1080 individually lit water jets, which pulse and dance in sequence. On hot spring and summer days, it becomes a busy urban beach. (www.kingscross.co.uk; Stable St; U King's Cross St Pancras)

London Canal Museum

MUSEUM

7 ◉ MAP P94, E2

This little museum on the Regent's Canal traces the history and everyday life of families living and working on London's impressively long and historic canal system. The exhibits in the stables upstairs are dedicated to the history of canal transport, including more recent developments such as the clean-up of the Lea River for the 2012 Olympic Games. The museum is housed in a warehouse dating from 1857, where ice was once stored in two deep wells. (☏020-7713 0836; www.canalmuseum.org.uk; 12-13 New Wharf Rd; adult/child £5/2.50; ⏰10am-4.30pm Tue-Sun & Mon bank holidays; U King's Cross St Pancras)

Charles Dickens Museum

MUSEUM

8 ◉ MAP P94, E5

The prolific writer Charles Dickens lived with his growing family in this handsome four-storey Georgian terraced house for a mere 2½ years (1837–39), but this is where his work really flourished, as here he completed *The Pickwick Papers*, *Nicholas Nickleby* and *Oliver Twist*. Each of the dozen rooms, some restored to their original condition, contains various memorabilia, including the study where you'll find the desk at which Dickens wrote *Great Expectations*. (☏020-7405 2127; www.dickensmuseum.com; 48-49 Doughty St; adult/child £9.50/4.50; ⏰10am-5pm Tue-Sun, plus Mon in Dec; U Russell Sq or Chancery Lane)

Eating

Chiltern Firehouse

MODERN EUROPEAN £££

9 ✖ MAP P94, A8

In-house restaurant of the hotel of the same name, itself occupying a beautiful red-brick firehouse from 1889, this splendidly dapper eatery offers opportunities to celeb-spot while enjoying the famed cooking of head chef Nuno Mendes. It's wildly popular, so book well ahead to enjoy dishes such as glazed hake with leek hearts and crab bisque flavoured with Chinese XO sauce. (☏020-7073 7676; www.chilternfirehouse.com; 1 Chiltern St; mains £32-42; ⏰7-10.30am, noon-3pm & 5.30-10.30pm Mon-Fri, 8am-3pm & 6-10.30pm Sat, 8am-3pm & 6-10pm Sun; 🛜; U Baker St or Bond St)

St Giles-in-the-Fields: a Litany of Miseries

Built in what used to be countryside between the City of London and Westminster, **St Giles-in-the-Fields** (Map p94, C8; ☏020-7240 2532; www.stgilesonline.org; 60 St Giles High St; ◷9am-4.30pm Mon-Fri; ⓊTottenham Court Rd) isn't much to look at but its history is a chronicle of London's most miserable inhabitants. The current structure (1733) is the third to stand on the site of an original chapel built in the 12th century to serve as a hospital for lepers.

Until 1547, when the hospital closed, prisoners on their way to be executed at the Tyburn Tree stopped at the church gate and sipped a large cup of soporific ale – their last refreshment – from St Giles's Bowl. From 1650, the prisoners were buried in the church grounds. It was also within the boundaries of St Giles that the Great Plague of 1665 took hold.

In Victorian times, it was London's worst slum, often mentioned in Dickens' novels. Today the drug users who hang out around the area make it feel like things haven't changed much.

An interesting relic in the church (northern side) is the plain white pulpit that was used for 40 years by John Wesley, the founder of Methodism.

Ruby Violet

ICE CREAM £

10 ✖ MAP P94, D1

Ruby Violet takes ice cream to the next level: flavours are wonderfully original (masala chai, raspberry and sweet potato) and toppings and hot sauces are shop-made. Plus, there's Pudding Club on Friday and Saturday nights, when you can dive into a mini baked Alaska or hot chocolate fondant. Eat in or sit by the fountain on Granary Sq (p97). (☏020-7609 0444; www.rubyviolet.co.uk; Midlands Goods Shed, 3 Wharf Rd; 1 scoop £3; ◷11am-7pm Mon & Tue, to 10pm Wed-Sun; ✱; ⓊKing's Cross St Pancras)

Roti King

MALAYSIAN £

11 ✖ MAP P94, B3

The neon sign pointing you in the direction of this pocket-sized basement restaurant doesn't look too promising, but the queues do. It's all about roti canai (£5 to £6.50), a flaky flatbread typical of Malaysia, served with fragrant bowls of curry or stuffed with tasty fillings. At last, a genuine budget option that isn't a sandwich or a salad. (☏020-7387 2518; https://rotiking.has.restaurant; 40 Doric Way; mains £5-7.50; ◷noon-3pm & 5-10.30pm Mon-Fri, noon-10.30pm Sat; ✈; ⓊEuston)

Caravan

INTERNATIONAL ££

12 🍴 MAP P94, C1

Housed in the lofty Granary Building, the King's Cross redevelopment's first tenant (2012) is a vast industrial-chic destination for tasty fusion bites from around the world. You can opt for several small plates to share tapas-style, or stick to main-sized dishes. The outdoor seating area on Granary Sq is especially popular on warm days, and cocktails are popular regardless of the weather. (📞020-7101 7661; www.caravanrestaurants.co.uk; 1 Granary Sq; small plates £7.50-9, mains £17.50-19; ⏱8am-10.30pm Mon-Fri, 10am-10.30pm Sat, to 4pm Sun; 🛜🍴; ⓊKing's Cross St Pancras)

Holborn Dining Room

MODERN BRITISH ££

13 🍴 MAP P94, E7

This masculine-feeling brasserie attached to the Rosewood London hotel – all reclaimed oak, antique mirrors and leather banquettes – serves up such delights as roast Suffolk pork belly, curried mutton pie and shrimp burger. But you'd be perfectly justified simply fronting up to the huge copper-topped bar to try one of 500-plus gins and 30 tonics on offer. (📞020-3747 8633; www.holborndiningroom.com; 252 High Holborn; mains £20-26; ⏱7am-10.30pm Mon-Fri, 7.30am-10.30pm Sat & Sun; ⓊHolborn)

North Sea Fish Restaurant

FISH & CHIPS ££

14 🍴 MAP P94, D4

Since 1977, the North Sea has set out to cook fresh fish and potatoes – a simple ambition in which it succeeds admirably. Jumbo-sized plaice, halibut, sole and other fillets are delivered daily, deep-fried or grilled, and served with plenty of chips. The original takeaway counter, an alternative to the simply furnished sit-down restaurant, is generally open 30 minutes longer each night. (📞020-7387 5892; www.northseafishrestaurant.co.uk; 7-8 Leigh St; mains £14-22; ⏱noon-2.30pm Tue-Sat, 5-10pm Mon-Sat, 5-9.30pm Sun; ⓊRussell Sq)

Bar Pepito

TAPAS £

15 🍴 MAP P94, D3

This tiny, intimate Andalusian bodega specialises in sherry and tapas. Novices fear not: the staff are on hand to advise. They're also experts at food pairings (top-notch ham and cheese selections). To go the whole hog, try a tasting flight of selected sherries with snacks to match. (📞020-7841 7331; www.camino.uk.com/restaurant/bar-pepito; 3 Varnishers Yard, The Regent Quarter; tapas £2.50-15; ⏱5pm-midnight Mon-Fri, 6pm-midnight Sat; ⓊKing's Cross St Pancras)

Drinking

Purl COCKTAIL BAR

16  MAP P94, A7

Purl is a fabulous underground drinking den – decked out in overstuffed vintage furniture in intimate nooks, and adorned with antique wood, stripped bricks and mementoes of glorious past epochs like the silent-film era. Foams, aromas, unlikely garnishes and bespoke glassware give cocktails old and new an air of discovery, while subdued lighting and conversation add to the mysterious air.

It's all seated, across a variety of rooms, and booking several days ahead is recommended – aim for Wednesday if you like live jazz.

(☎020-7935 0835; www.purl-london. com; 50-54 Blandford St; ⏰5-11.30pm Mon-Thu, to midnight Fri & Sat; Ⓤ Baker St or Bond St)

London Cocktail Club COCKTAIL BAR

17  MAP P94, A7

Pendant bar lights, graffitied walls, bright clutter and raucous atmosphere give a New York vibe to this snug basement saloon just north of Oxford St. If you prefer to drink seated, arrive early or hire the private booth: it gets pretty packed. The cocktail menu is about the length of the Brooklyn Bridge, with plenty of house specials. (☎020-7580 1960; www.londoncocktailclub. co.uk/goodge-street; 61 Goodge

Charles Dickens Museum (p98)

St; ⏱4.30pm-midnight Mon-Sat; Ⓤ Goodge St)

Queen's Larder

PUB

18 🚇 MAP P94, D6

This cheery local favourite takes its name from Queen Charlotte, who previously stored food here for her husband George III, during his nearby treatment for insanity. The food today is *very* English (think Spam with chips and beans) and served daily from noon to 3pm, while the snug bar is augmented by a few outside tables and an upstairs dining room. (☎020-7837 5627; www.queenslarder. co.uk; 1 Queen Sq; ⏱11.30am-11pm Mon-Fri, noon-11pm Sat, noon-10.30pm Sun; Ⓤ Russell Sq)

Museum Tavern

PUB

19 🚇 MAP P94, D7

Inaugurated in 1723, this storied pub has refreshed scholars from the British Museum's Reading Room including Karl Marx, George Orwell, Sir Arthur Conan Doyle and JB Priestley. Handsomely adorned with original late-Victorian etched glass, lead lighting and woodwork, it's popular with academics, students and travellers alike. It also serves pub classics from pies and burgers to a Sunday roast. (☎020-7242 8987; 49 Great Russell St; ⏱11am-11.30pm Mon-Thu, to midnight Fri & Sat, noon-10.30pm Sun; 📶; Ⓤ Holborn or Tottenham Court Rd)

Princess Louise

PUB

20 🚇 MAP P94, E8

The gorgeous ground-floor saloon of this Sam Smith's pub, dating from 1872, boasts pressed-tin ceilings, handsome tiling, etched mirrors and 'snob screens' (swivelling panels concealing genteel Victorian drinkers from bar staff and other workers), and a stunning central horseshoe bar. The original Victorian wood partitions provide plenty of private nooks, and typical pub food is served from noon to 2.30pm Monday to Friday, and 6pm to 8.30pm Monday to Thursday (mains £8 to £12). (☎020-7405 8816; 208 High Holborn; ⏱11am-11pm Mon-Fri, noon-11pm Sat, noon-6.45pm Sun; Ⓤ Holborn)

Lamb

PUB

21 🚇 MAP P94, E5

Its curved mahogany bar topped with etched-glass 'snob screens' and its walls hung with antique lithographs, the Lamb seems the Platonic ideal of a London pub. Enjoy your Young's bitter on the deep-green upholstered banquettes, or in the walled beer garden in fine weather. (☎020-7405 0713; www.thelamblondon.com; 94 Lamb's Conduit St; ⏱11am-11pm Mon-Wed, to midnight Thu-Sat, noon-10.30pm Sun; Ⓤ Russell Sq)

London's Bewildering Postcodes

The 20 arrondissements in Paris spiral clockwise from the centre in a lovely, logical fashion. Not so London's postcodes. Look at a map and you may be thinking: why does SE23 border SE6?

When they were introduced in 1858, the postcodes were fairly clear, with all the compass points represented, along with an east and west central (EC and WC). But not long afterwards, NE was merged with E and S with SE and SW, and the problems began. The real convolution came during WWI when a numbering system was introduced for inexperienced sorters (regular employees were off fighting in 'the war to end all wars'). No 1 was the centre of each zone, but other numbers related to the alphabetical order of the postal districts' names. Thus anything starting with a letter near the beginning of the alphabet, like Chingford in East London, would get a low number (E4), even though it was miles from the centre at Whitechapel (E1), while Poplar, which borders Whitechapel, got E14. It wasn't designed to confuse regular punters, but it does.

Euston Tap
BAR

22 MAP P94, B4

This specialist drinking spot inhabits a monumental stone structure on the approach to Euston station. Craft-beer devotees can choose between 15 cask ales, 28 keg beers and 150 brews by the bottle. Grab a seat on the pavement, take the tight spiral staircase upstairs or buy a bottle to take away. (020-3137 8837; www.eustontap.com; 190 Euston Rd; noon-11.30pm Mon-Thu, to midnight Fri & Sat, to 10pm Sun; U Euston)

Entertainment

Scala
LIVE MUSIC

23 MAP P94, E3

Opened in 1920 as a cutting-edge golden-age cinema, Scala slipped into porn-movie hell in the 1970s, only to be reborn as a club and live-music venue in the early 2000s. It's one of the top places in London to catch an intimate gig and is a great dance space, too, hosting a diverse range of club nights. (020-7833 2022; www.scala.co.uk; 275 Pentonville Rd; cover £10-35; U King's Cross St Pancras)

The Place
DANCE

24 ⭐ MAP P94, C4

The birthplace of modern British dance is one of London's most exciting cultural venues, still concentrating on challenging and experimental choreography. Behind the late-Victorian terracotta facade you'll find a 300-seat theatre, an arty, creative cafe atmosphere and a dozen training studios. (☎020-7121 1100; www.theplace.org.uk; 17 Duke's Rd; Ⓤ Euston Sq)

Shopping

London Review Bookshop
BOOKS

25 🔒 MAP P94, D7

The flagship bookshop of the *London Review of Books* fortnightly literary journal doesn't put faith in towering piles of books and slabs on shelves, but offers a wide range of titles in a handful of copies only. It often hosts high-profile author talks, and there's a charming cake store where you can leaf through your new purchases. (☎020-7269 9030; www.londonreviewbookshop.co.uk; 14 Bury Pl; ⏱10am-6.30pm Mon-Sat, noon-6pm Sun; Ⓤ Holborn)

Daunt Books
BOOKS

26 🔒 MAP P94, A6

An original Edwardian bookshop, with oak panels, galleries and gorgeous skylights, Daunt is one of London's loveliest bookshops. There are several Daunt outlets but none as gorgeous. (☎020-7224 2295; www.dauntbooks.co.uk; 83 Marylebone High St; ⏱9am-7.30pm Mon-Sat, 11am-6pm Sun; Ⓤ Baker St)

Forbidden Planet
COMICS

27 🔒 MAP P94, C8

Forbidden Planet is a trove of comics, sci-fi, horror and fantasy literature, as well as action figures and toys, spread over two floors. It's an absolute dream for anyone into manga comics, off-beat genre titles, and sci-fi and fantasy memorabilia. (☎020-7420 3666; www.forbiddenplanet.com; 179 Shaftesbury Ave; ⏱10am-7pm Mon & Tue, to 7.30pm Wed, Fri & Sat, to 8pm Thu, noon-6pm Sun; Ⓤ Tottenham Court Rd)

Gay's the Word
BOOKS

28 🔒 MAP P94, D5

The UK's first and only specifically gay and lesbian bookstore, this London institution has been selling LGBTIQ+ works since 1979. It has a superb selection and a genuine community spirit, bolstered by frequent discussion groups. (☎020-7278 7654; www.gaystheword.co.uk; 66 Marchmont St; ⏱10am-6.30pm Mon-Sat, 2-6pm Sun; Ⓤ Russell Sq)

James Smith & Sons Umbrellas
FASHION & ACCESSORIES

29 🔒 MAP P94, C8

Nobody makes and stocks such elegant umbrellas (not to mention walking sticks and canes) as this place. It's been fighting the British weather from the

London Review Bookshop

same address since 1857, and London's ever-present drizzle means they'll hopefully be here for years to come. Prices reflect the quality. The beautiful old-school signage is worth a photo stop alone. (📞020-7836 4731; www.james-smith.co.uk; 53 New Oxford St; 🕑10am-5.45pm Mon, Tue, Thu & Fri, 10.30am-5.45pm Wed, 10am-5.15pm Sat; Ⓤ Tottenham Court Rd)

Explore ⊛
St Paul's &
City of London

London's historic core is a tale of two cities: packed with weekday office workers and eerily quiet at weekends. For most of its history, the entire city was enclosed between sturdy walls that were only dismantled in the 18th century. The current millennium has seen daring skyscrapers sprout around the Square Mile, but the essential sights have been standing for hundreds of years: St Paul's Cathedral and the Tower of London.

The Short List

○ **Tower of London (p112)** *Discovering almost 1000 years of history and marvelling at the Crown Jewels.*

○ **St Paul's Cathedral (p108)** *Walking in awed reverence below the cathedral's mighty dome.*

○ **Museum of London (p118)** *Tracing the history of the city, from Roman origins to 21st-century metropolis.*

○ **Sky Garden (p118)** *Marvelling at London's ultra-modern architecture from the penthouse urban jungle.*

○ **City Social (p120)** *Elevating dinner to new heights with Michelin-starred cuisine in a 24th-floor lookout.*

Getting There & Around

Ⓤ The City is served by seven Tube lines and the DLR.

🚌 Numerous bus routes pass through the City's main streets.

⛴ Thames Clippers operates boats from Tower Millennium Pier and Blackfriars Pier.

Neighbourhood Map on p116

St Paul's Cathedral (p108) MARIA AVVAKUMOVA/SHUTTERSTOCK ©

Top Experience 📷

Stand in Awe at St Paul's Cathedral

Sir Christopher Wren's gleaming grey-domed masterpiece is the City of London's most magnificent building. Built between 1675 and 1710 after the Great Fire destroyed its predecessor, St Paul's was the first triple-domed cathedral in the world. Its vast, climbable cupolas still soar triumphantly over Ludgate Hill, offering sublime London panoramas, and some of the country's most celebrated citizens are interred in its crypt.

◎ MAP P116, D4

📞 020-7246 8357

www.stpauls.co.uk

St Paul's Churchyard

adult/child £20/8.50

🕐 8.30am-4.30pm Mon-Sat

U St Paul's

Dome

Wren wanted to construct a dome that was imposing on the outside but not disproportionately large on the inside. The solution was to build it in three parts: a plastered brick inner dome, a nonstructural lead outer dome and a brick cone between them holding it all together, one inside the other. This unique structure, inspired by St Peter's Basilica in the Vatican, made the cathedral Wren's tour de force. Climb up the 528 stairs, thankfully in three stages, to access the cathedral's galleries.

Whispering Gallery

Enter through the door on the western side of the southern transept, where 257 steps lead to the interior walkway around the dome's base, 30m above the floor. This is the Whispering Gallery.

Stone Gallery & Golden Gallery

Climbing another 119 steps brings you to the Stone Gallery, an outdoor viewing platform 53m above the ground, obscured by pillars and other safety measures. The remaining 152 iron steps to the Golden Gallery are steeper and narrower than below but are worth the effort. From here, 85m above London, you can enjoy superb 360-degree views of the city.

Interior

At a time of anti-Catholic fervour, it was controversial to build a Roman-style basilica rather than using the more familiar Gothic style. St Paul's interiors were more reflective of Protestant tastes, being relatively unadorned, with large clear windows. The statues and mosaics seen today were added later.

★ Top Tips

o There's no charge to attend a service, but not all areas of the cathedral are accessible. To hear the cathedral choir, go to the 11.30am Sunday Eucharist, or to Evensong (5pm Monday to Saturday and 3.15pm Sunday).

o Audio guides are included in the price of admission.

o Free 1½-hour guided tours depart four times a day (10am, 11am, 1pm and 2pm): reserve a place at the tour desk, just past the entrance.

✗ Take a Break

For an on-site pick-me-up, visit the cafe or tearoom in the crypt. If you prefer not to eat in church, Ivy Asia (p122) dishes up OTT fusion plates with views of the cathedral through its floor-to-ceiling windows. Cheaper chain restaurants can be found in the One New Change (p119) shopping centre.

Duke of Wellington Memorial

In the north aisle of the vast nave, you'll find the grandiose Duke of Wellington Memorial (1912), which took 54 years to complete. The Iron Duke's horse Copenhagen originally faced the other way, but it was deemed unfitting that a horse's rear end should face the altar. In contrast, beneath the dome is an elegant epitaph written for Wren by his son: *Lector, si monumentum requiris, circumspice* (Reader, if you seek his monument, look around you).

The Light of the World & the Quire

In the north transept chapel is William Holman Hunt's celebrated painting *The Light of the World* (1851–53), which depicts Christ knocking at a vine-covered door that, symbolically, can only be opened from within. In the heart of the cathedral, you'll find the spectacular quire (or chancel) – its ceilings and arches dazzling with colourful mosaics – and the high altar. The ornately carved choir stalls by Dutch-British sculptor Grinling Gibbons on either side of the quire are exquisite, as are the ornamental wrought-iron gates, separating the aisles from the altar, by French Huguenot Jean Tijou.

American Memorial Chapel

Walk around the altar, with its massive gilded oak baldacchino (canopy) with barley-twist columns, to the American Memorial Chapel, commemorating the 28,000 Americans based in Britain who lost their lives during WWII.

St Paul's Cathedral

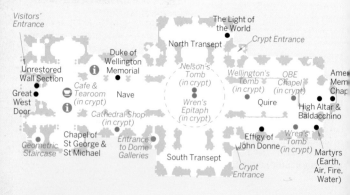

Cathedral Floor & Crypt

Crypt & OBE Chapel

On the eastern side of both the north and south transepts are stairs leading down to the crypt and the OBE Chapel, where services are held for members of the Order of the British Empire. The crypt has memorials to around 300 of Britain's great and good, including Florence Nightingale, TE Lawrence (better known as Lawrence of Arabia) and Winston Churchill. Those actually buried here include the Duke of Wellington, Vice Admiral Horatio Nelson, Christopher Wren and the painters Joshua Reynolds, John Everett Millais, JMW Turner and William Holman Hunt.

Also in the crypt are the cathedral's cafe, tearoom, gift shop and toilets.

Churchyard & Surrounds

A statue of Queen Anne (the reigning monarch when St Paul's was built) stands at the cathedral steps, her gilded crown, sceptre and orb glinting in the sun. The figures at her feet represent Britannia, North America, France and Ireland. Made by sculptor Louis Auguste Malempré in 1886, it's a replica of the Francis Bird original from 1712.

Outside the north transept, the simple, squat and round People of London Memorial, honours the 32,000 civilians killed (and 50,000 seriously injured) during WWII.

Fifth Time Lucky

London's mother church has stood on this site since 604 CE. Wren's cathedral is the fifth incarnation, built to replace the soaring Gothic-style Old St Paul's after it was destroyed in the Great Fire in 1666. Old St Paul's was both longer and taller than Wren's version.

Tours Behind the Scenes

Audio guides are included in the price of a ticket, but it's worth signing up for two guided tours of St Paul's to get access to usually off-limits areas.

Free 1½-hour guided tours cover most of the same ground as the audio guide, with the added bonus of being able to enter the quire for a better look at the ceiling mosaics. These tours cannot be booked online or in advance, so check in at the tour desk as soon as you arrive.

The Triforium Tour (£8) runs much less frequently but includes the chance to descend the Geometric Staircase (the Divination Stairwell from the *Harry Potter* films), take in the BBC-exclusive view of the nave that's usually reserved for camera crews, see Wren's original oak model of St Paul's and visit the astounding library.

Top Experience

See the Crown Jewels at the Tower of London

With a history as bloody as it is fascinating, the Tower is London's most absorbing sight. Begun during the 11th-century reign of William the Conqueror, this royal fortress is in fact a castle containing 22 towers, and has served as a palace, observatory, armoury, mint, zoo, prison and execution site.

◎ MAP P116, H5

☏ 020-3166 6000

www.hrp.org.uk/tower-of-london

Petty Wales

adult/child £28.90/14.40

🕑 9am-4.30pm Tue-Sat, 10am-4.30pm Sun & Mon

Ⓤ Tower Hill

Tower Green & Scaffold Site

What looks at first glance like a peaceful, almost village-like slice of the Tower's inner ward, is actually one of its bloodiest. Those who have met their fate at the Scaffold Site include two of Henry VIII's wives, Anne Boleyn and Catherine Howard; 16-year-old Lady Jane Grey, who fell foul of Henry's daughter Mary I after her family attempted to have her crowned queen; and Robert Devereux, Earl of Essex, once a favourite of Elizabeth I. Just west of the Scaffold Site is Beauchamp Tower (1280), where high-ranking prisoners left behind unhappy inscriptions and other graffiti.

Chapel Royal of St Peter ad Vincula

On the northern edge of Tower Green is the 16th-century Chapel Royal of St Peter ad Vincula (St Peter in Chains), a rare surviving example of ecclesiastical Tudor architecture. Those buried here include three queens (Anne Boleyn, Catherine Howard and Lady Jane Grey) and two saints (Thomas More and John Fisher). A third saint, Philip Howard, was also interred here before his body was moved to Arundel in southern England.

Crown Jewels

To the east of the Chapel Royal and north of the White Tower is Waterloo Barracks, home of the Crown Jewels, which are in a very real sense priceless. The queue to get in can be extremely long, but once inside, you'll be dazzled by lavishly bejewelled sceptres, orbs and crowns. Two moving walkways take you past crowns and other coronation regalia, including the platinum crown of the late Queen Mother, Elizabeth, which is set with the 106-carat Koh-i-Nûr (Persian for 'Mountain of Light') diamond, and the Sovereign's Sceptre with Cross topped with the drop-shaped 530-carat Great Star of Africa diamond (also known as Cullinan I).

★ Top Tips

o Don't feel obliged to pay the additional Gift Aid price (which allows UK citizens to pass on a tax break to the Tower) on top of what is already a hefty admission fee.

o Purchasing your ticket online (valid for seven days from the date selected) saves even more money and avoids queues at the ticket booth.

o Start with a free Yeoman Warder tour, which is a great way to familiarise yourself with the site.

o Don't leave your visit too late in the day; set aside three to four hours to see everything.

✕ Take a Break

Within the Tower walls, the **New Armouries Cafe** serves British standards in a self-serve cafeteria-style setting.

BrewDog Tower Hill (p124) is a short walk away, dishing up pizzas, burgers and salads that are best washed down with a craft beer brewed on-site.

A bit further on, exhibited on its own, is the centrepiece: the Imperial State Crown, set with 2868 diamonds (including the 317-carat Second Star of Africa, also known as Cullinan II), sapphires, emeralds, rubies and pearls. It's worn by the monarch at the State Opening of Parliament.

White Tower

At the heart of the site is the oldest building left standing in the whole of London. Constructed from stone as a fortress in the 1070s, the White Tower was the original Tower of London – its current name arose after Henry III whitewashed it in the 13th century. Standing just 27m high, it's not exactly a skyscraper by modern standards, but in the Middle Ages it would have dwarfed the wooden huts surrounding the castle walls and intimidated the peasantry.

Most of its interior is given over to the Royal Armouries collection of cannons, guns, suits of chain mail, and armour for men and horses. One of the most remarkable exhibits in the Line of Kings are Henry VIII's suits of armour, including one made for him when he was a dashing 24-year-old and another when he was a bloated 50-year-old with a waist measuring 129cm.

Chapel of St John the Evangelist

This 11th-century chapel, with its vaulted ceiling, rounded archways and 14 stone pillars, is a fine example of Norman architecture and was also used as a national record office.

Bloody Tower

The Bloody Tower (1225) takes its nickname from the princes in the Tower – 12-year-old Edward V and his younger brother, Richard – who were held here by their uncle and later thought to have been murdered to annul their claims to the throne. The blame is usually laid (notably by Shakespeare) at the feet of their uncle, Richard III. A small exhibition recreates the study of explorer Sir Walter Raleigh – a repeat prisoner here – and looks at torture at the Tower, with gruesome replica devices such as the Rack and the Scavenger's Daughter.

Medieval Palace

Inside St Thomas's Tower (built 1275–79) is a reconstructed hall and bedchamber from the time of Edward I. Adjoining Wakefield Tower (1220–40) was built by Edward's father, Henry III. It has been furnished with a replica throne and other decor to give an impression of how it might have looked.

Wall Walk

The huge inner wall of the Tower was added by Henry III from 1220 to improve the castle's defences. The Wall Walk allows you to tour its eastern and northern edge and the towers that punctuate it. Start at the Salt Tower and continue through the Broad Arrow Tower and Constable Tower, containing small displays on weapons and the Peasants' Revolt. The Martin Tower, which housed the Crown Jewels from 1669 to 1841,

Tower of London Traditions

Yeomen Warders

The iconic Yeomen Warders, dressed in their signature red-trimmed navy uniform, have been guarding the Tower of London since the 15th century. Though their roles today are mostly ceremonial, they must have served at least 22 years in the British Armed Forces to qualify for the job. The Yeomen Warders are better known as the Beefeaters, a nickname that's been around since at least the 17th century. Its origins are unknown, although it's thought to be because of the large rations of beef – then a luxury – once given to them as part of their salary. But another tradition still lives on: warders receive a bottle of Beefeater Gin on their birthday as part of an old arrangement with its producers for use of their image on the bottle.

Ravens

Superstition has it that if the Tower of London's six resident ravens ever leave, then the kingdom will fall. Call it silly, but the 350-year-old rumour is thought to have persisted since the reign of Charles II – who lived through the plague, the Great Fire *and* the execution of his father – and the Tower's guardians today still aren't taking any chances. The six required birds, plus one spare, are kept in an on-site aviary and are dutifully cared for by the in-house ravenmaster.

Ceremony of the Keys

Said to be the oldest military ceremony in the world, the elaborate locking of the Tower's main gates has been performed nightly without fail for more than 700 years. The Ceremony of the Keys begins precisely at 9.53pm, and it's all over by 10.05pm. Even when a bomb hit the Tower of London during the Blitz, the ceremony was delayed by only 30 minutes. Tickets to the Ceremony of the Keys cost £1 and must be booked online (www.hrp.org.uk) far in advance.

contains an exhibition about the original coronation regalia with some of the older crowns on show.

Along the north wall, the Brick Tower has a fascinating display on the royal menagerie, including stories of a tethered polar bear that swam and fished in the Thames. The Bowyer Tower has exhibits about the Duke of Wellington, while the Flint Tower is devoted to the castle's role during WWI.

Tours

While they officially guard the Tower, the Yeomen Warders' main role these days is as tour guides. Entertaining 45-minute-long tours leave from the bridge near the main entrance every 30 minutes until 3.30pm (2.30pm in winter). Make this your first stop before exploring the Tower on your own; it's included in the price of your entry ticket.

For reviews see

0   500 m
0   0.25 miles

E   F   G   H

Leonard St

City Rd

Tabernacle St

Paul St

Scrutton St

Holywell Row

Great Eastern St

Redchurch St

Bethnal Green Rd

Sclater St

1

Shoreditch High St

Commercial St

Quaker St

Brick La

Bunhill Row

Chiswell St

Worship St

Curtain Rd

Appold St

Lamb St

Hanbury St

2

Ropemaker St

Silk St

South Pl

Wilson St

Sun St

Exchange Sq

Brushfield St

Fournier St

Moor La

Moorgate

Finsbury Circus

Liverpool St

Artillery La

Commercial St

Wentworth St

3

Fore St

Moorgate

Guildhall t Gallery

Basinghall St

London Wall

Blomfield St

Liverpool St

Bishopsgate

Houndsditch

Middlesex St

Coulston St

Petticoat Lane Market

Coleman St

Moorgate

Wormwood St

×10

7

Throgmorton Ave

Old Broad St

×9

St Mary Axe

×19

Aldgate

Aldgate High St

Mansell St

4

Bank of England Museum

15

6

Threadneedle St

Leadenhall St

Jewry St

Minories

Princes St

Cornhill

12 18

Gracechurch St

Lime St

Fenchurch St

Crutched Friars

Tower Gateway DLR

Poultry

King William St

Walbrook

Queen

Bank

Fenchurch St

Mark La

Tower Hill

East Smithfield

5

Cannon St

Monument

Monument to the Great Fire of London

5

Eastcheap

2

Sky Garden

Great Tower St

21

Tower Hill

Tower Bridge Approach

Lower Thames St

Cousin La

Cannon St

River Thames

London Bridge

London Bridge City Pier

Tower Millennium Pier

Tower of London

Tower Bridge Exhibition

8

6

Clink St

Thames Path

Borough High St

Duke Hill St

London Bridge

Tooley St

St Thomas

E   F   G   H

Sights

Museum of London

MUSEUM

1 ◉ MAP P116, D3

Romp through 450,000 years of London history at this entertaining and educational museum, one of the capital's finest. Exhibiting everything from a mammoth's jaw circa 200,000 BCE to Oliver Cromwell's death mask and the desperate scrawls of convicts on a cell from Wellclose Prison, interactive displays and reconstructed scenes transport visitors from Roman Londinium and Saxon Lundenwic right up to the 21st-century metropolis. (☏020-7001 9844; www.museumoflondon.org. uk; 150 London Wall; admission free; ☻10am-6pm; Ⓤ Barbican)

Sky Garden

VIEWPOINT

2 ◉ MAP P116, F5

The ferns, fig trees and purple African lilies that clamber up the final three storeys of the 'Walkie Talkie' skyscraper are mere wallflowers at this 155m-high rooftop garden – it's the extraordinary 360-degree views of London that make this vast, airport-terminal-like space so popular. The Sky Garden has front-row seats overlooking the Shard and vistas that gallop for miles east and west. Visits must be booked online in advance; the garden space also includes a restaurant, a brasserie and three bars. (☏020-7337 2344; www.skygarden.london; 20 Fenchurch St; admission free; ☻10am-6pm Mon-Fri, 11am-9pm Sat & Sun; Ⓤ Monument)

Sky Garden

St Mary Aldermary CHURCH

3 ◉ MAP P116, D4

A Christoper Wren reconstruction, the church of St Mary Aldermary (1682) is unusual for the architect: it was built in Gothic style, and it's the only surviving church in the City of London of this type. Be prepared to spend some time gawping at the ceiling of the columned nave, covered in gleaming white plaster fan vaulting that's offset by the polished wood pews and medieval-style blood-red floor tiles. **Host Cafe** livens up the scene from its espresso bar in the apse. (☑020-7248 9902; Bow Lane; ⏱7.30am-4.30pm Mon-Fri; Ⓤ Mansion House)

Barbican ARCHITECTURE

4 ◉ MAP P116, D2

The architectural value of this sprawling post-WWII brutalist housing estate divides Londoners, but the Barbican remains a sought-after living space as well as the City's preeminent cultural centre. Public spaces include a quirky **conservatory** (Level 3; admission free; ⏱noon-5pm Sun) and the Barbican Centre theatres (p125), cinema, and two art galleries: **Barbican Art Gallery** (Level 3; ⏱noon-6pm Mon & Tue, to 9pm Wed-Fri, 10am-9pm Sat, to 6pm Sun) and the **Curve** (Level 1; admission free; ⏱11am-8pm Sat-Wed, to 9pm Thu & Fri).

Navigating the Barbican, designed to be a car-free urban neighbourhood, requires reliance on a network of elevated paths

Free Views

Designed by French architect Jean Nouvel, **One New Change** (Map p116, D4; ☑020-7002 8900; www.onenew change.com; 1 New Change; ⏱10am-6pm Mon-Wed & Sat, to 8pm Thu & Fri, noon-6pm Sun; Ⓤ St Paul's) is a shopping centre housing mainly high-street brands, but take the lift to the 6th floor and an open viewing platform will reward you with up-close views of the dome of St Paul's Cathedral and out over London.

that didn't quite come to fruition. Find your bearings on an architecture tour (adult/child £12.50/10). (☑020-7638 4141; www.barbican.org. uk; Silk St; Ⓤ Barbican)

Monument to the Great Fire of London MONUMENT

5 ◉ MAP P116, F5

Designed by Christopher Wren, this immense Doric column of Portland stone is a reminder of the Great Fire of London in 1666, which destroyed 80% of the city. It stands 62m high, the distance from the bakery in Pudding Lane where the fire is thought to have started. Although Lilliputian by today's standards, the Monument towered over London when it was built. Climbing up the column's 311 spiral steps still provides great views thanks to its central location. ([phone] 020-7403 3761; www.themonument.org.uk; Fish St Hill; adult/child £5/2.50, incl Tower Bridge Exhibition £12/5.50; [time] 9.30am-5.30pm; [U] Monument)

Bank of England Museum

MUSEUM

6 [icon] MAP P116, F4

This surprisingly interesting museum explores the evolution of money and the history of the venerable Bank of England, founded in 1694 by a Scotsman. Its centrepiece is a reconstruction of architect John Soane's original Bank Stock Office. Don't miss the chance to get your hands on a hefty 13kg solid-gold bar, worth more than £570,000. ([phone] 020-3461 5545; www.bankofengland.co.uk/museum; Bartholomew Lane; admission free; [time] 10am-5pm Mon-Fri; [U] Bank)

Guildhall Art Gallery

GALLERY

7 [icon] MAP P116, E3

The City of London has had centuries to acquire an impressive art collection, which it has shown off since 1885. The original gallery was destroyed in the Blitz, and when the site was redeveloped in 1985, the remains of a Roman amphitheatre (c 70 CE) were discovered, so the gallery was redesigned to incorporate the ruins. The 4500-piece collection is particularly strong on London scenes and Victorian art, including significant pre-Raphaelite works by John Everett Millais and Dante Gabriel Rossetti. ([phone] 020-7332 3700; www.cityoflondon.gov.uk/guild

hallgalleries; Guildhall Yard; admission free; [time] 10am-5pm Mon-Sat, noon-4pm Sun; [U] Bank)

Tower Bridge Exhibition

MUSEUM

8 [icon] MAP P116, H6

The inner workings of Tower Bridge can't compare with its exterior magnificence, but this geeky exhibition tries to bridge that gap with details of the construction and access to the Victorian steam-powered machinery that once raised the bascules. Archive footage at the start of the exhibition shows the bridge lifting for the first time, and girders in the South Tower show the bridge's original drab chocolate-brown paint job. Walking on the glass floors 42m above the River Thames is a highlight. ([phone] 020-7403 3761; www.towerbridge.org.uk; Tower Bridge; adult/child £9.80/4.20, incl Monument £12/5.50; [time] 9.30am-5pm; [U] Tower Hill)

Eating

City Social

BRITISH £££

9 [icon] MAP P116, F3

City Social pairs sublime skyscraper views from its 24th-floor digs with delicate Michelin-starred cuisine. The interior is all art deco–inspired low-lit glamour. If you don't want to splash out on the full menu, opt for the bar, **Social 24**, which has longer hours and a compelling menu of nibbles (don't miss the goats'-cheese churros with truffle-infused honey). ([phone] 020-7877 7703;

The Great Fire of London

London had for centuries been prone to fire, as nearly all buildings were constructed from wood and roofed with thatch, but the mother of all blazes broke out on 2 September 1666 in a bakery in Pudding Lane close to London Bridge. It didn't seem like much to begin with – the mayor himself dismissed it as something 'a woman might piss out' before going back to bed – but the unusual autumn heat combined with rising winds meant the fire raged out of control for four days, reducing 80% of London to ash. Only eight people died (officially at least), but most of medieval London was obliterated. The fire finally stopped at Pye Corner in Smithfield, then on the very edge of London, not before destroying 89 churches, including St Paul's Cathedral, and more than 13,000 houses, leaving tens of thousands of people homeless. The Monument to the Great Fire of London (p119) stands near the fire's start, and a small statue of a podgy naked boy, the **Golden Boy of Pye Corner** (Map p116, C3; cnr Cock Lane & Giltspur St; U St Paul's), marks the point where it burnt out.

www.citysociallondon.com; Tower 42, 25 Old Broad St; mains £26-37; ⏰noon-2.30pm & 6-10.30pm Mon-Fri, 5-10.30pm Sat; U Bank)

Duck & Waffle
BRITISH ££

10 ✖ MAP P116, G3

London tends to have an early bedtime, but Duck and Waffle is the best restaurant that's ready to party all night. Survey the kingdom from the highest restaurant in town (on the 40th floor) over a helping of the namesake dish: a fluffy waffle topped with a crispy leg of duck confit and a fried duck egg, drenched in mustard-seed maple syrup. (☎020-3640 7310; www.duckandwaffle.com; Heron Tower, 110 Bishopsgate; mains £14-44; ⏰24hr; 🛜; U Liverpool St)

Miyama
JAPANESE ££

11 ✖ MAP P116, C4

There's a sense of a well-kept secret about this authentic Japanese restaurant, tucked away in a basement of a nondescript building (enter from Knightrider St). Come at midday for the good-value set-menu lunch that could include sashimi, tempura, tonkatsu and teriyaki, and sit at the sushi or teppanyaki bar for culinary drama. (☎020-7489 1937; www.miyama-restaurant.co.uk; 17 Godliman St; mains £13.50-30; ⏰11.30am-2.30pm & 5.45-9.30pm Mon-Fri; U St Paul's)

Simpsons Tavern
BRITISH £

12 ✖ MAP P116, F4

'Old school' doesn't even come close to describing Simpsons, a

City institution since 1757. Huge portions of traditional British grub are served to diners in dark-wood and olive-green booths. Save space for the tavern's famous stewed-cheese dessert. (☎020-7626 9985; www.simpsonstavern.co.uk; Ball Ct, 38½ Cornhill; mains £9.75-15.80; ☺8.30-10.30am Tue-Fri & noon-3.30pm Mon-Fri; Ⓤ Bank)

Ivy Asia
ASIAN £££

13 ✖ MAP P116, D4

Newly opened Ivy promises to inject some late-night life into this part of the City, and it's well on its way with a nightly resident DJ, an extensive range of Japanese whiskies, and OTT menu items like black-truffle dumplings that come sprinkled in gold leaf. The glowing green floor is made from semiprecious stones, and St Paul's gleams through the huge windows. (☎020-3971 2600; www.theivyasia.com; 20 New Change; mains £13.50-48; ☺11.30am-2.30am Mon-Sat, to 12.30am Sun; Ⓤ St Paul's)

Drinking

Oriole
COCKTAIL BAR

14 🍸 MAP P116, C3

Down a darkened alley through the eerie evening quiet of Smithfield Market is an unlikely spot for one of London's best cocktail bars, but the journey of discovery is the theme at speakeasy-style Oriole. The cocktail menu, divided into Old World, New World and the Orient, traverses the globe,

with out-of-this-world ingredients including clarified octopus milk, strawberry tree curd and slow-cooked chai palm. (☎020-3457 8099; www.oriolebar.com; E Poultry Ave; ☺6-11pm Mon to 2am Tue-Sun; Ⓤ Farringdon)

Nickel Bar
COCKTAIL BAR

15 🍸 MAP P116, E4

There's something Great Gatsby–ish about the Ned hotel: the elevated jazz pianists, the vast verdite columns, the classy American-inspired cocktails. Of all the public bars inside this magnificent former banking hall, the Nickel Bar soaks up the atmosphere best. Inspired by the glamorous art-deco saloons and the ocean-liner-era elegance, this is timeless nightcap territory. (☎020-3828 2000; www.thened.com/restaurants/the-nickel-bar; 27 Poultry; ☺8am-2am Mon-Fri, 9am-3am Sat, to midnight Sun; 🛜; Ⓤ Bank)

Viaduct Tavern
PUB

16 🍸 MAP P116, C3

Opened in 1869, the Viaduct Tavern is one of the only remaining Victorian gin palaces in the City, with etched glass panes, blood-red embossed vines crawling along the ceiling, and even the old cashier's booth where drink tokens were purchased (because the bar staff weren't trusted with cash). The tavern still specialises in gin, and a selection of house-made infusions beckons from behind the bar.

The Viaduct is said to be one of London's most haunted pubs, perhaps not a surprise given its proximity to the notorious, now demolished Newgate Prison; there are still jail cells in the pub's basement. (☏ 020-7600 1863; www.viaducttavern.co.uk; 126 Newgate St; ⏱ 10am-11pm Mon-Fri, noon-9pm Sat; 🛜; Ⓤ St Paul's)

Merchant House   COCKTAIL BAR

17 🚇 MAP P116, E4

This well-hidden bar, on a seemingly forgotten alleyway off pedestrian-only Bow Lane, has some 600 whiskies, 400 rums and 400 gins. Don't worry about a novel-size drink list, though: instead, the master mixologists will whip up a custom concoction based on your alcohol of choice and one of five taste palettes, such as umami, tropical, coastal or smoke. (www.merchanthouse.bar; 13 Well Ct; ⏱ 3pm-1am Mon-Fri, 4pm-1am Sat; Ⓤ Mansion House)

Counting House   PUB

18 🚇 MAP P116, F4

With its grand wooden staircase and painted ceilings edged with gold-coloured crown moulding, this pub, part of the Fuller's chain, is still every bit as dignified as when it opened as Prescott's Bank in 1893. Suited City folk crowd around the elegantly curved central bar under the domed skylight for the range of traditional cask ales and speciality pies. (☏ 020-7283 7123; www.the-counting-house.com; 50 Cornhill; ⏱ 8am-11pm Mon-Fri, 11am-11pm Sat, to 9pm Sun; 🛜; Ⓤ Bank)

Searcys at the Gherkin   BAR

19 🚇 MAP P116, G4

The top two floors of the iconic Gherkin skyscraper were once reserved as a private members' club, but now anyone dressed to impress is invited up. Cocktails in the 40th-floor bar under the oculus roof with 360-degree views of the City are a sight to behold. (☏ 0330 107 0816; www.searcysathegherkin.co.uk; 30 St Mary Axe; ⏱ 11am-11pm Mon-Sat, 10am-4pm Sun; Ⓤ Aldgate)

Viaduct Tavern

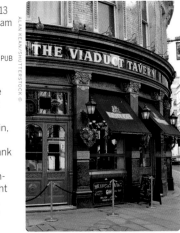

City of London Distillery

COCKTAIL BAR

20 MAP P116, B4

The first gin distillery to be opened in the City for nearly 200 years, this small-batch micro-distillery has brought back the art of 'mother's ruin'. Sip on a classic G&T while peeking at the shiny vats behind glass windows at the back of the bar, or if you can't choose just one, opt for a gin flight. The distillery also runs tours and gin-making classes. (☎020-7936 3636; www.cityoflondondistillery.com; 22-24 Bride Lane; ☉2-11pm Mon-Sat; ☒City Thameslink, ☒Blackfriars)

BrewDog Tower Hill

CRAFT BEER

21 MAP P116, G5

The ubiquitous but delicious Scottish brewery recently opened this new outpost half-buried under an office block steps from the Tower of London. The 33 craft-beer taps, featuring BrewDog's own beers – some of which are brewed on-site

Barbican Centre

Top City of London...

Meals with a view Every London skyscraper now seems to come affixed with a high-altitude bar or restaurant. Get a taste of the high life at art-deco-inspired City Social (p120).

Old-style boozers Though they tend to keep bankers' hours, the City's old-school restaurants and pubs are some of the most atmospheric and historic in town. Viaduct Tavern (p123), a former Victorian gin palace, is one of the best.

Culture hub The City isn't London's cultural core, but the Barbican Centre (below) is a powerhouse of innovative theatre, music and art.

– as well as the greatest hits from other brewers, ensure the place never goes dry. (☎020-7929 2545; www.brewdog.com; 21 Great Tower St; ☿noon-11pm Sun-Wed, to midnight Thu-Sat; 🛜; Ⓤ Tower Hill)

Entertainment

Barbican Centre   PERFORMING ARTS

 2 ⭐ MAP P116, D2

You'll get as lost in the astounding programme as you will in the labyrinthine brutalist building. Home to the London Symphony Orchestra, the BBC Symphony Orchestra and the Royal Shakespeare Company, the Barbican Centre is the City's premier cultural venue. It hosts concerts, theatre and dance performances, and screens indie films and Hollywood blockbusters at the cinema on Beech St. (☎020-7638 8891; www.barbican.org.uk; Silk St; ☿box office 10am-9pm Mon-Sat, noon-8pm Sun; Ⓤ Barbican)

Shopping

London Silver Vaults   ANTIQUES

23 🔒 MAP P116, A3

For one of London's oddest shopping experiences, pass through security and descend 12m into the windowless subterranean depths of the London Silver Vaults, which house the largest collection of silver for sale in the world. The 30-odd independently owned shops, each entered through thick bank-safe-style doors, offer vintage Victorian and Georgian silver, cufflinks, candleholders, goblets and much more. Despite its Chancery Lane address, the entrance is on Southampton Buildings. (☎020-7242 3844; www.silvervaultslondon.com; 53-64 Chancery Lane; ☿9am-5.30pm Mon-Fri, to 1pm Sat; Ⓤ Chancery Lane)

Explore ⊚
Tate Modern
& South Bank

South Bank is a must-visit area for art lovers, theatre-goers and architecture buffs, with the recently revamped Tate Modern and iconic brutalist buildings to explore. Come for the Thames views, great food markets, dollops of history, a smattering of street culture, and some excellent pubs, bars and restaurants on and around the riverfront.

The Short List

○ **Tate Modern (p128)** *Getting a grip on modern art inside a magnificently renovated former power station.*

○ **Shakespeare's Globe (p141)** *Getting a Bard's-eye view of Elizabethan theatrics at this authentic recreation of the 16th-century original.*

○ **Borough Market (p134)** *Stimulating your taste buds on a gastronomic tour of a gourmet market.*

○ **Imperial War Museum (p134)** *Hearing the challenging stories behind conflicts past and present.*

○ **Southbank Centre (p135)** *Losing yourself in the concrete corridors of this brutalist arts complex.*

Getting There & Around

Ⓤ The Jubilee Line is the main artery through South Bank, but the area can also be reached on the Bakerloo, Northern, and Waterloo and City lines.

🚌 The RV1 bus runs from Tower Gateway to Covent Garden via South Bank and Bankside, linking the main sights.

⚓ Thames Clippers boats stop at London Bridge City Pier, Bankside Pier and London Eye Pier.

Neighbourhood Map on p132

Tate Modern (p128) COWARDLION/SHUTTERSTOCK ©

Top Experience 📷

Get with the Trends at Tate Modern

Tate Modern is a phenomenally successful modern- and contemporary-art gallery housed in an imposing former power station on the riverside. The 10-storey Blavatnik Building extension, opened in 2016, increased exhibition space by 60%.

◉ MAP P132, D2

📞 020-7887 8888

www.tate.org.uk

Bankside

admission free

🕙 10am-6pm Sun-Thu, to 10pm Fri & Sat

Ⓤ Southwark

Natalie Bell Building

The original gallery lies inside what was once the boiler house for the Bankside Power Station. Now called the Natalie Bell Building in recognition of a local community activist, the structure is an imposing sight: a 200m-long building made of 4.2 million bricks. Don't miss the views of the River Thames and St Paul's Cathedral from the 6th-floor cafe.

Turbine Hall

The first space to greet you as you pour down from the Holland St entrance is the astounding 3300-sq-metre Turbine Hall (pictured). Originally housing the power station's humongous electricity generators, this vast area has become the commanding venue for large-scale installations and temporary exhibitions. The annual commission aims to make art more accessible and has led to popular and often interactive pieces, such as Kara Walker's *Fons Americanus*, a 13m-tall working fountain that highlights the history of the slave trade; a full-on playground of three-person swings installed by Danish art collective Superflex; and a maze of geometric gardens called *Empty Lot* by Abraham Cruzvillegas, which took soil from parks around London and then watered it for six months to see if anything grew. Note that if you enter from the riverside doors, you'll end up on the more muted level 1, but stairs lead down to the main floor of the Turbine Hall.

Blavatnik Building

The Tate Modern extension that opened in 2016 echoes the original building in appearance: it is also constructed of brick, although these are slightly lighter and have been artistically laid out in a lattice to let light in.

The interior is stark, with raw, unpolished concrete vaguely reminiscent of brutalist buildings, and the exhibition space is fantastic, giving the collection the room it deserves to shine.

★ Top Tips

○ The Natalie Bell Building and the Blavatnik Building are connected at levels 0, 1 and 4; pick up a map (£1) at one of the stands near the entrances to make navigating easier.

○ For the most scenic of culture trips, take the RB2 riverboat service between **Bankside Pier** (www.thamesclippers.com; one way adult/child £8.70/4.35) outside Tate Modern and Millbank Pier near its sister museum, Tate Britain (p56).

✕ Take a Break

Borough Market (p134), overflowing with small shops, food stalls cooking in close quarters and wholesale greengrocers catering to London's top-end restaurants, is a 10-minute walk east along the river. All-vegetarian Tibits (p139) puts a hip spin on cafeteria-style dining.

Viewing Gallery: Level 10

Take the lift to level 10 for sweeping panoramic views of the city. The combination indoor-outdoor space means it's still worth a visit in bad weather.

The Tanks

Huge subterranean tanks once stored oil for the power station, and these unusual circular spaces are now dedicated to showing live art, performance, installation and film.

Permanent Collection

The Tate Modern's permanent collection is free to visit and is arranged by both theme and chronology on levels 2 and 4 of the Natalie Bell Building and on levels 0, 3 and 4 of the Blavatnik Building. The emphasis in the latter is on art from the 1960s onwards.

More than 60,000 works are on constant rotation, which can be frustrating if you'd like to see one particular piece, but keeps it thrilling for repeat visitors. Helpfully, you can check the excellent website (www.tate.org.uk/search) to see whether a specific work is on display – and where.

Curators have at their disposal paintings by Georges Braque, Henri Matisse, Piet Mondrian, Andy Warhol, Mark Rothko and Jackson Pollock, as well as pieces by Joseph Beuys, Barbara Hepworth, Damien Hirst, Rebecca Horn and Claes Oldenburg.

A great place to begin is the Start Display on level 2 of the

Tate of the Art

Swiss architects Herzog & de Meuron scooped the prestigious Pritzker Architecture Prize for their transformation of the empty Bankside Power Station, which closed in 1981. Strokes of genius included leaving the building's single central 99m-high chimney, adding a two-storey glass box onto the roof and using the cavernous Turbine Hall as a dramatic exhibition space.

Natalie Bell Building: this small, specially curated taster features some of the best-loved works in the collection and gives visitors useful pointers for understanding modern art.

Tours

Three free 45-minute tours run every day through Tate Modern's permanent exhibitions, providing an introduction to the gallery before moving on to a specific section. These talks start at noon, 1pm and 2pm on level 4 of the Natalie Bell Building.

Special Exhibitions

With the opening of the Blavatnik Building, Tate Modern has increased the number of special exhibitions it hosts. You will find the exhibits on level 3 of the Natalie Bell Building and level 2 of the Blavatnik Building; all are subject to admission charges, which vary by exhibition.

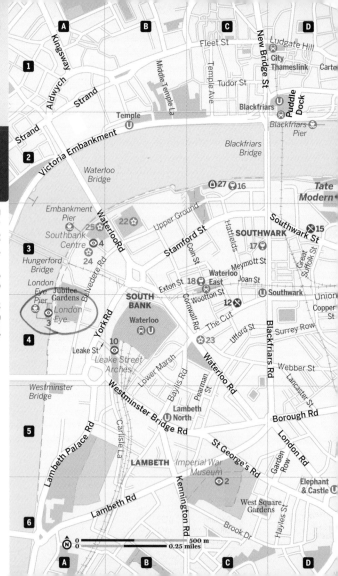

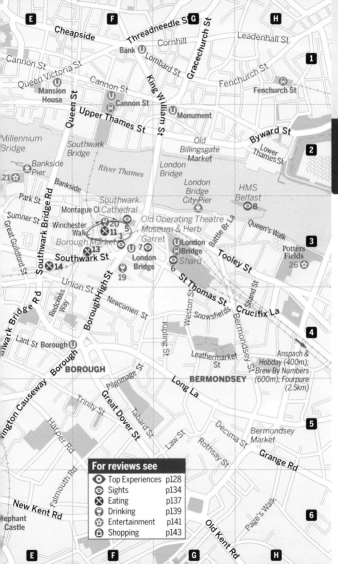

E
Cheapside
F
Threadneedle St
G
Cornhill
Leadenhall St
H
1

Cannon St
Queen Victoria St
Bank U
Lombard St
Gracechurch St
Fenchurch St

Mansion House U
Cannon St
Cannon St U
King William St
Monument U

Upper Thames St
Queen St
Old Billingsgate Market
Fenchurch St

Millennium Bridge
Southwark Bridge
London Bridge
Byward St
Lower Thames St
2

Bankside Pier
River Thames
London Bridge

21

Park St
Bankside
London Bridge City Pier
HMS Belfast
8

Montague Cl
Southwark Walk
Southwark Cathedral
Old Operating Theatre Museum & Herb Garret
Queen's Walk
3

Sumner St
Winchester Walk
20
5
11
1
London Bridge U
Battle Br La
Potters Fields
26

Borough Market
13
7
London Bridge
Shard
Tooley St
4

Great Guildford St
Southwark Bridge Rd
Southwark St
14
19
6
St Thomas St
Shand St
Anspach & Hobday (400m); Brew By Numbers (600m); Fourpure (2.5km)

Union St
Redcross Way
Borough High St
Newcomen St
Weston St
Snowsfields
Crucifix La
Bermondsey St
5

Lant St
Borough U
Kipling St
Leathermarket St
Long La
BERMONDSEY
Decima St
Bermondsey Market

wark Bridge Rd
ngton Causeway
Borough
BOROUGH
Pilgrimage St
Trinity St
Great Dover St
Tabard St
Law St
Rothsay St
Grange Rd

Harper Rd
Falmouth Rd
New Kent Rd
ephant Castle
Old Kent Rd
6

For reviews see

◎	Top Experiences	p128
◉	Sights	p134
✕	Eating	p137
🍷	Drinking	p139
★	Entertainment	p141
🛍	Shopping	p143

E
F
G
H

Sights

Borough Market
MARKET

1 MAP P132, F3

For a thousand years, a market has existed at the southern end of London Bridge, making this still-busy ancient gathering point a superb spectacle. Overflowing with small shops, food stalls and wholesale greengrocers catering to London's top-end restaurants, Borough Market makes a delicious lunch stop, afternoon grazing session or pure dinner-party inspiration. Expect it to be crowded, even on days with limited traders. (www.borough market.org.uk; 8 Southwark St; ⊙full market 10am-5pm Wed & Thu, to 6pm Fri, 8am-5pm Sat, limited market 10am-5pm Mon & Tue; Ⓤ London Bridge)

Imperial War Museum
MUSEUM

2 MAP P132, C6

Fronted by an intimidating pair of 15-inch naval guns and a piece of the Berlin Wall, this riveting museum is housed in what was the Bethlem Royal Hospital, a psychiatric facility also known as Bedlam. Although the museum's focus is on military action involving British or Commonwealth troops, largely during the 20th century, it also covers war in the wider sense. Must-see exhibits include the state-of-the-art First World War galleries and Witnesses to War in the forecourt and atrium. (☎020-7416 5000; www.iwm.org.uk; Lambeth Rd; admission free; ⊙10am-6pm; Ⓤ Lambeth North)

London Eye

London Eye VIEWPOINT

3 MAP P132, A4

Standing 135m high in a fairly flat city, the London Eye is the world's largest cantilevered observation wheel and affords views 25 miles in every direction (as far as Windsor Castle), weather permitting. Each ride – or 'flight' – takes a gracefully slow 30 minutes. The London Eye is the focal point of the capital's midnight New Year's Eve fireworks display and one of the UK's most popular tourist attractions; book tickets online in advance for a slight discount or fast-track entry to jump the queue. (www.londoneye.com; near County Hall; adult/child £28/23; 10am-8.30pm, reduced hours in winter; U Waterloo or Westminster)

Southbank Centre ARTS CENTRE

4 MAP P132, A3

Southbank Centre, Europe's largest space for performing and visual arts, is made up of three brutalist buildings that stretch across seven riverside hectares: Royal Festival Hall (p142), Queen Elizabeth Hall (p143) and **Hayward Gallery** (11am-7pm Mon, Wed, Sat & Sun, to 9pm Thu). With cafes, restaurants, shops and bars, this complex is always a hub of activity, from the singing lift up to the 6th floor to teenage skateboarders doing tricks in the Undercroft. In summer, the fountains and artificial beach on the waterfront are a hit with youngsters. (020-3879 9555;

Strolling South Bank

Exploring South Bank on foot is best; if you're pressed for time, allocate at least half a day to walk from Westminster Bridge to London Bridge along the River Thames, with stops at the London Eye, Southbank Centre, Tate Modern, Shakespeare's Globe and Borough Market.

www.southbankcentre.co.uk; Belvedere Rd; 10am-11pm; U Waterloo)

Southwark Cathedral CATHEDRAL

5 MAP P132, F3

Southwark Cathedral, a mostly Victorian construction but with a history dating back many centuries earlier, was the nearest church to what was once the only entry point into the city, London Bridge. The cathedral is relatively small, but the Gothic arched nave is impressive, as is the 16th-century saint-filled High Altar Screen. Tombs and memorials are scattered throughout, including the tomb of John Gower and an alabaster Shakespeare Memorial. Evensong takes place at 5.30pm on weekdays, 4pm on Saturdays and 3pm on Sundays. (020-7367 6700; www.cathedral. southwark.anglican.org; Montague Cl; 9am-5pm Mon-Fri, 9.30am-3.45pm & 5-6pm Sat, 12.30-3pm & 4-6pm Sun; U London Bridge)

Like a Local in South Bank

Neighbourhood local The views are grand, but the riverside is clogged with chains. Instead, head inland for locally loved back-street boozers, such as the Kings Arms (p140).

Hotel bars Londoners aren't staying overnight, but you'll sure find them at hip hotel watering holes, such as Lyaness (p139) and Hoxton's Seabird (p140).

Abandoned arches London's once derelict railway arches are undergoing huge regeneration projects: seek out street art in the Leake Street Arches (opposite) or follow the still-in-progress Low Line to the restaurants in the Old Union Yard Arches and Flat Iron Square (p139).

Shard

VIEWPOINT

 6 ◉ MAP P132, G3

Puncturing the skies above London, the dramatic splinter-like form of the Shard has become an icon of the city and is one of the tallest buildings in Europe. The scene from the 244m-high viewing platforms on floors 69 and 72 is like none other in town, but it comes at an equally lofty price; book online in advance for a potential discount. Premium tickets come with a good-weather guarantee, meaning you might be able to return for free. (📞0844 499 7111; www.theviewfromtheshard.com; Joiner St; adult/child from £25/20; ⌚10am-9pm; ⓊLondon Bridge)

Old Operating Theatre Museum & Herb Garret

MUSEUM

7 ◉ MAP P132, F3

This unique museum, 32 steps up a spiral stairway in the tower

of St Thomas Church (1703), is the unlikely home of Britain's oldest surviving operating theatre. Rediscovered in 1956, the attic was used by the apothecary of St Thomas' Hospital to store medicinal herbs. The museum looks back at the horror of 19th-century medicine, all pre-anaesthetic and pre-antiseptic. You can browse the natural remedies, including snail water for venereal disease, and recoil at the fiendish array of amputation knives and blades. (📞020-7188 2679; www.oldoperating theatre.com; 9a St Thomas St; adult/child £6.50/3.50; ⌚2-5pm Mon, 10.30am-5pm Tue-Fri, noon-4pm Sat & Sun; ⓊLondon Bridge)

HMS Belfast

SHIP

8 ◉ MAP P132, H3

HMS *Belfast* is a magnet for kids of all ages. This large, light cruiser – launched in 1938 – served in WWII, helping to sink the Nazi battleship

Sand shelling the Normandy coast on D-Day, and in the Korean War. Its 6-inch guns could bombard a target 12 miles distant. Displays offer great insight into what life on board was like, in peacetime and during military engagements. Excellent audio guides, included in the admission fee, feature anecdotes from former crew members. (www.iwm.org.uk/visits/hms-belfast; Queen's Walk; adult/child £19/9.50; ⏰10am-4pm; Ⓤ London Bridge)

Millennium Bridge BRIDGE

9 ◎ MAP P132, E2

The elegant steel, aluminium and concrete Millennium Bridge staples the south bank of the Thames, in front of Tate Modern, to the north bank, at Peter's Hill below St Paul's Cathedral. The low-slung frame designed by Sir Norman Foster and Anthony Caro looks spectacular, particularly when lit up at night, and the view of St Paul's from South Bank has become one of London's iconic images. (Ⓤ Blackfriars)

Leake Street Arches AREA

10 ◎ MAP P132, B4

A grungy road under Waterloo station seems an unlikely place to find art, theatre and restaurants, but Leake St is the latest of London's railway arches to get the redevelopment treatment. Opened by famous street artist Banksy in 2008, the walls of the 200m-long Leake Street Tunnel are covered from floor to ceiling with some

seriously impressive spray-painted works, and new taggers turn up daily. Banksy's work is long gone, but you can watch today's artists painting over what was put up yesterday. (www.leakestreetarches. london; Leake St; Ⓤ Waterloo)

Eating

Padella ITALIAN £

Come hungry for the best pasta this side of Italy. Padella (see 1 ◎ Map p132, F3) is a small, energetic bistro specialising in handmade noodles, inspired by the owners' extensive culinary adventures. The portions are small, which means that you can (and should!) have more than one dish. The queue is always long; download the WalkIn app to join it virtually and head to the pub.

The dishes on offer are often switched up, but the menu mainstay of *pici cacio e pepe* is a must. (www.padella.co; 6 Southwark St; dishes £4-12.50; ⏰noon-3.45pm & 5-10pm Mon-Sat, noon-3.45pm & 5-9pm Sun; 🍴; Ⓤ London Bridge)

Arabica Bar & Kitchen MIDDLE EASTERN ££

11 ✖ MAP P132, F3

Set in a brick-lined railway arch, Arabica specialises in classic Middle Eastern favourites served mezze-style, so round up a group to sample and share as many of the small plates as possible. Stars of the menu include creamy baba ganoush, made with perfectly smoked aubergine and saffron

Flat Iron Square

yoghurt, and charcoal-grilled lamb kebab. (📞020-3011 5151; www. arabicabarandkitchen.com; 3 Rochester Walk, Borough Market; dishes £6-14; 🕙noon-10.30pm Mon-Fri, 9am-10.30pm Sat, 10am-9.30pm Sun; 🏃; Ⓤ London Bridge)

Skylon
EUROPEAN £££

Named after the original structure in this location for the 1951 Festival of Britain, Skylon (see 24 ⭐ Map p132, A3) brings the 1950s into the modern era, with retro-futuristic decor (trendy then, trendier now) and a season-driven menu of contemporary British cuisine. But its biggest selling point might be the floor-to-ceiling windows that offer magnificent views of the Thames and the city. (📞020-7654 7800; www.skylon-restaurant.co.uk;

3rd fl, Royal Festival Hall, Southbank Centre, Belvedere Rd; mains £16.50-34; 🕙noon-11pm Mon-Fri, 11.30am-3pm & 5-11pm Sat, 11.30am-10.30pm Sun; 🛜♿; Ⓤ Waterloo)

Anchor & Hope
GASTROPUB ££

12 🍽 MAP P132, C4

Started by former chefs from nose-to-tail pioneer St John (p188), the Anchor & Hope is a quintessential gastropub: elegant but not formal, serving utterly delicious European fare with a British twist. The menu changes daily, but it could include grilled sole served with spinach, or roast rabbit with green beans in a mustard-and-bacon sauce. Bookings are taken for Sunday lunch only. (📞020-7928 9898; www.anchorandhopepub. co.uk; 36 The Cut; mains £12.40-19.40;

⊙5-11pm Mon, 11am-11pm Tue-Sat, 12.30-3.15pm Sun; Ⓤ Southwark)

Casa do Frango   PORTUGUESE ££

13 ⊗ MAP P132, F3

Forget your notions of Nando's: Casa do Frango kicks peri-peri up a notch in its cool plant-filled upstairs space steps away from Borough Market. Frango, Algarvian-style charcoal-grilled chicken brushed with peri-peri sauce, is the star of the menu, which also includes regionally flavoured sharing plates. Seek out the hidden door to the dimly lit speakeasy for after-dinner drinks. (www.casadofrango.co.uk; 32 Southwark St; dishes £6-10; ⊙noon-3pm & 5-10.30pm Mon-Thu, noon-11pm Fri & Sat, to 10pm Sun; Ⓤ London Bridge)

Flat Iron Square   FOOD HALL £

14 ⊗ MAP P132, E3

This industrial-chic food court weaves through seven railway arches and has commandeered the surrounding outdoor space to offer a foodie hub for the indecisive. Want to dine on gyoza, pizza, pad thai, buttermilk chicken or Mediterranean salads? No need to pick just one. Flat Iron also hosts events, including vintage markets and themed nights. Hours and prices vary for individual traders. (☏020-3179 9800; www.flatiron square.co.uk; Flat Iron Sq; ⊙noon-midnight Mon-Sat, 10.30am-10pm Sun; ✈; Ⓤ London Bridge)

Tibits   VEGETARIAN ££

15 ⊗ MAP P132, D3

This all-vegetarian cafe puts a hip spin on cafeteria-style dining. A rotating selection of innovative veggie and vegan dishes are laid out along a DIY service counter, where you can load up on helpings of salad, curry, risotto and more, and then your plate is weighed at the till. Its location and relaxed atmosphere make it a perfect post–Tate Modern refuelling stop. (☏020-7202 8370; www.tibits.co.uk; 124 Southwark St; plates priced by weight; ⊙7.30am-10pm Mon-Wed, to 11pm Thu & Fri, 11.30am-11pm Sat, to 10pm Sun; ✈; ▣Blackfriars, Ⓤ Southwark)

Drinking

Lyaness   COCKTAIL BAR

16 ⊗ MAP P132, C2

Six months after Dandelyan was named the best bar in the world, renowned mixologist Ryan Chetiya-wardana closed it down. Reincarnated in that space with much the same atmosphere and modus operandi is Lyaness. The bar prides itself on unusual ingredients; look out for vegan honey, whey liqueur and onyx, a completely new type of alcohol. (☏020-3747 1063; www.lyaness.com; Sea Containers, 20 Upper Ground; ⊙4pm-1am Mon-Wed, noon-2am Thu-Sat, to 12.30am Sun; 🛜; Ⓤ Southwark)

Bermondsey Beer Mile

London's craft-beer revival is in full swing, and Bermondsey is at its epicentre. Some two dozen breweries and taprooms have established themselves along a disjointed 2km stretch of industrial railway arches. Most are working breweries and limit hours to the weekends. Set aside a Saturday to sample the best of the city's beer scene.

Favourite stops along the Bermondsey Beer Mile include **Anspach & Hobday** (020-8617 9510; www.anspachandhobday.com; 118 Druid St; 5-10pm Fri, 10.30am-10pm Sat, 1-6pm Sun; Ⓤ Bermondsey), which pours its flagship dark coffee-chocolate porter among a handful of others; ever-experimental **Brew By Numbers** (www.brewbynumbers.com; 75-79 Enid St; 5-10pm Wed & Thu, 4-10.30pm Fri, noon-10pm Sat, to 6pm Sun; Ⓤ Bermondsey), with its 'scientific' branding and penchant for exploring new styles and refashioning old ones; and the revamped taproom of **Fourpure** (020-3744 2141; www.fourpure.com; 25 Bermondsey Trading Estate; noon-8pm Tue & Sun, to 10pm Wed-Fri, 11am-8pm Sat; Ⓡ South Bermondsey), complete with suspended egg chairs, trailing vines and, of course, plenty of suds to choose from with its 43 craft-beer taps.

Seabird ROOFTOP BAR

17 MAP P132, C3

South Bank's latest rooftop bar might also be its best. Atop the new Hoxton Southwark hotel, sleek Seabird has palm-filled indoor and outdoor spaces where you can spy St Paul's from the comfort of your wicker seat. If you're hungry, seafood is the speciality, and the restaurant claims London's longest oyster list. (020-7903 3050; www.seabirdlondon.com; Hoxton Southwark, 40 Blackfriars Rd; noon-midnight Mon-Thu, to 1am Fri, 11am-1am Sat, to midnight Sun; Ⓤ Southwark)

Kings Arms PUB

18 MAP P132, C3

Set on old-school Roupell St, this charming backstreet neighbourhood boozer serves up a rotating selection of traditional ales and bottled beers. The after-work crowd often makes a pit stop here before heading to Waterloo station, spilling out onto the street at peak hours. The farmhouse-style room at the back of the pub serves decent Thai food. (020-7207 0784; www.thekingsarmslondon.co.uk; 25 Roupell St; 11am-11pm Mon-Sat, noon-10.30pm Sun; Ⓤ Waterloo)

George Inn PUB

L9 MAP P132, F3

This magnificent galleried coaching inn is the last of its kind in London. The building, owned by the National Trust, dates from 1677 and is mentioned in Charles Dickens' *Little Dorrit*. In the evenings, the picnic benches in the huge cobbled courtyard fill up (no reservations); otherwise, find a spot in the labyrinth of dark rooms and corridors inside. (☎020-7407 2056; www.nationaltrust.org.uk/george-inn; 77 Borough High St; ⏰11am-11pm Mon-Thu, to midnight Fri & Sat, noon-10.30pm Sun; Ⓤ London Bridge)

Rake PUB

20 MAP P132, F3

Run by the founders of hop emporium Utobeer, Rake has an astonishing selection of suds, including rare brews impossible to find anywhere else in town. Guided by the helpful bar staff, you can't go wrong. It's a teensy place, and it's always busy; the decking outside is especially popular. (☎020-7407 0557; www.facebook.com/TheRakeSE1; 14 Winchester Walk; ⏰noon-11pm Mon-Thu, 11am-11pm Fri, 10am-11pm Sat, noon-10pm Sun; Ⓤ London Bridge)

Aqua Shard BAR

If you want a view from the Shard (p136) for the price of a cocktail, find your way up to the 31st floor and into this gorgeous three-storey bar and restaurant (see 6 ◉ Map p132, G3). The lofty ceiling adds awe to the London panoramas shining through the high sloping glass walls. Only the restaurant takes bookings, so expect a wait if you come at peak drinking hours. (☎020-3011 1256; www.aquashard.co.uk; 31st fl, The Shard, 31 St Thomas St; ⏰10.30am-1am Sun-Thu, to 3am Fri & Sat; Ⓤ London Bridge)

Entertainment

Shakespeare's Globe THEATRE

21 MAP P132, E2

One of the most famous playhouses in the world, Shakespeare's Globe will knock your theatrical socks off. This dutifully authentic reconstruction will transport theatre-goers back to Elizabethan times, with hard wooden seats and a central floor space open to the

Craft beer at Fourpure

CK TRAVELS/SHUTTERSTOCK ©

elements (cushions and ponchos are on sale). Groundling tickets are just £5 for every performance, but you're required to stand through the whole show. (📞020-7401 9919; www.shakespearesglobe.com; 21 New Globe Walk; ⏰box office 10am-6pm; Ⓤ Blackfriars, London Bridge)

National Theatre
THEATRE

22 ⭐ MAP P132, B3

The nation's flagship theatre delivers up to 25 shows every year across its three venues inside this brutalist block. Even if you're not here for a show, you can explore the foyers, which contain a bookshop, restaurants, bars and exhibition spaces. Get behind the scenes on a tour, including going backstage, a deep-dive into the building's architecture and an experience with the costume team. (📞020-7452 3000; www.nationaltheatre.org.uk; Upper Ground; Ⓤ Waterloo)

Old Vic
THEATRE

23 ⭐ MAP P132, C4

This 1000-seater nonprofit theatre celebrated its 200th season in 2018 and continues to bring eclectic programming occasionally bolstered by big-name actors, such as Daniel Radcliffe. (📞0344 871 7628; www.oldvictheatre.com; The Cut; Ⓤ Waterloo)

Royal Festival Hall
CONCERT VENUE

24 ⭐ MAP P132, A3

The 2700-capacity Royal Festival Hall is one of the best places in London to hear modern and

Old Vic

classical music, poetry and spoken-word performances. The hall has four resident orchestras, including the London Philharmonic Orchestra and the London Sinfonietta. (📞020-3879 9555; www.southbankcentre.co.uk/venues/royal-festival-hall; Southbank Centre, Belvedere Rd; 🛜; Ⓤ Waterloo)

Queen Elizabeth Hall
LIVE PERFORMANCE

25 ⭐ MAP P132, A3

Queen Elizabeth Hall has a full programme of gigs, chamber orchestras, dance performances and opera throughout the year, on a smaller scale than the nearby Royal Festival Hall that's also part of Southbank Centre (p135). The space reopened in 2018 after a three-year refurb. In summer, don't miss the plant-strewn **cafe-bar** (🕑 noon-9pm Apr–mid-Jun & Sep-Oct, 10am-10.30pm mid-Jun–Aug) on the roof. (📞020-3879 9555; www.southbankcentre.co.uk/venues/queen-elizabeth-hall; Southbank Centre, Belvedere Rd; Ⓤ Waterloo)

Bridge Theatre
THEATRE

26 ⭐ MAP P132, H3

London's first new major theatre in 80 years, Bridge Theatre seats 900 in a cool, modern space and focuses on new productions, with the occasional classic thrown in. (📞0333 320 0051; www.bridgetheatre.co.uk; 3 Potters Fields Park; Ⓤ London Bridge)

All South Bank is a Stage

Across the river and away from the naysayers in the buttoned-down City of London, playful South Bank has been a destination for entertainment since the Middle Ages. This area has a dense concentration of theatres, including the reconstructed Shakespeare's Globe (p141), as well as Britain's largest cinema screen. The many venues inside Southbank Centre (p135) host performing arts and live music. Don't miss the chance to catch a show in the area.

Shopping

Suck UK
GIFTS & SOUVENIRS

27 🔒 MAP P132, C2

Suck UK's artsy, quirky gifts are so funny that you'll want to keep them for yourself. London's weather will likely call for an umbrella that changes colour when wet, or you can pick up a few items for home, perhaps a cat scratcher that looks like a DJ turntable or a doormat that says 'come in' but when turned upside down reads 'go away'. (📞020-7928 0855; www.suck.uk.com; ground fl, Oxo Tower Wharf; 🕑 10am-7pm Mon-Sat, to 5.30pm Sun; Ⓤ Waterloo)

Explore

Kensington Museums

Well-groomed Kensington is among London's handsomest neighbourhoods. It has three fine museums – the Victoria & Albert Museum, the Natural History Museum and the Science Museum – plus excellent dining and shopping, graceful parklands and grand period architecture.

The Short List

o **Victoria & Albert Museum (p146)** *Discovering an encyclopaedic A to Z of decorative and design works while admiring the astonishing architecture.*

o **Natural History Museum (p150)** *Gaping at the awe-inspiring stonework and inexhaustible collection.*

o **Science Museum (p156)** *Grappling with the complexities of the world and the cosmos in this electrifying museum.*

o **Hyde Park (p157)** *Picnicking in London's green lung and exploring its sights and verdant scenery.*

o **Harrods (p165)** *Big-time shopping – or perhaps just big-time window-shopping!*

Getting There & Around

U Hyde Park Corner, Knightsbridge and South Kensington (Piccadilly Line) and South Kensington, Sloane Sq and High St Kensington (Circle & District Lines).

Handy routes include 74, 52 and 360.

Neighbourhood Map on p154

Hyde Park (p157) | WEI HUANG/SHUTTERSTOCK ©

Top Experience 📷
Stroll among Artworks at Victoria & Albert Museum

Specialising in decorative art and design, the V&A's unparalleled collection is displayed in a setting as inspiring as the sheer diversity and rarity of its exhibits. Its original aims were the 'improvement of public taste in design' and 'applications of fine art to objects of utility'. In this endeavour, the museum continues to wow, astonish and inform.

◎ MAP P154, E5

📞 020-7942 2000

www.vam.ac.uk

Cromwell Rd, SW7

admission free

🕙 10am-5.45pm Sat-Thu, to 10pm Fri

Ⓤ South Kensington

Collection

Through 146 galleries, the museum houses the world's greatest collection of decorative arts, from ancient Chinese ceramics to modernist architectural drawings, Japanese swords, cartoons by Raphael, gowns from the Elizabethan era, ancient jewellery, a Sony Walkman – and much, much more. The museum is open till 10pm on Friday evenings, although the number of open galleries is reduced.

Entrance

Enter under the stunning blue-and-yellow blown-glass chandelier by Dale Chihuly. (If the 'Grand Entrance' on Cromwell Rd is too busy, enter around the corner on Exhibition Rd, or from the tunnel in the basement, if arriving by Tube.)

Level 0

The street level is mostly devoted to art and design from India, China, Japan, Korea and Southeast Asia, as well as European art. One of the museum's highlights is the **Cast Courts** in rooms 46a and 46b, containing staggering plaster casts collected in the Victorian era, such as Michelangelo's David, acquired in 1858. More European excellence is on display in room 48a in the form of the Raphael Cartoons.

The **TT Tsui (China) Gallery** (rooms 44 and 47e) displays lovely pieces, including a beautifully lithe wooden statue of Guanyin (a Mahayana bodhisattva) seated in a regal *lalitasana* pose from 1200 CE. Within the subdued lighting of the **Japan Gallery** (room 45) stands a fearsome suit of armour in the Domaru style. More than 400 objects are within the **Islamic Middle East Gallery** (room 42), including ceramics, textiles, carpets, glass and woodwork from the 8th century up to the years before WWI. The exhibition's highlight is the gorgeous mid-16th-century Ardabil Carpet. Soft lights illuminate the carpet on the hour and every half hour.

★ Top Tips

o Visit late nights on Fridays, when there are fewer visitors.

o Work out what you want to see and how to reach it before you visit.

o Grab a museum map (£1) from the information desk.

o If it gets too exhausting, remember the museum is free, so you can always come back for more.

✗ Take a Break

Perfect for a breather, the V&A Cafe (p162) is a picture; the afternoon tea is a choice occasion.

For scrummy Lebanese cuisine, leg it to **Comptoir Libanais** (☎020-7225 5006; www.comptoirlibanais. com; 1-5 Exhibition Rd, SW7; mains £10-15; ⏱8.30am-midnight Mon-Sat, to 10.30pm Sun; 🛜🍴), around the corner from South Kensington Tube station.

John Madejski Garden & Refreshment Rooms

For fresh air, the landscaped John Madejski Garden is a lovely shaded inner courtyard. Cross it to reach the original Refreshment Rooms (Morris, Gamble and Poynter Rooms), dating from the 1860s and redesigned by McInnes Usher McKnight Architects (MUMA), who also renovated the Medieval and Renaissance galleries (1350–1600) to the right of the Grand Entrance.

Level 1 & 3

The **British Galleries**, featuring every aspect of British design from 1500 to 1900, are divided between levels 2 (1500–1760) and 4 (1760–1900). Level 4 also boasts the **Architecture Gallery** (rooms 127 to 128a), which vividly describes architectural styles via models and videos, and the spectacular, brightly illuminated **Contemporary Glass Gallery** (room 129).

Level 2

The **Jewellery Gallery** (room 91) is outstanding; the mezzanine level – accessed via the glass-and-perspex spiral staircase – glitters with jewel-encrusted swords, watches and gold boxes. The **Photographs Centre** (rooms 100 and 101) is one of the nation's best, with access to over 500,000 images collected since the mid-19th century. **Design Since 1945** (room 76) celebrates design classics from a 1985 Sony credit-card radio to a 1992 Nike 'Air Max' shoe, Peter Ghyczy's Garden Egg Chair from 1968 and the now ubiquitous selfie stick.

Level 4

Among the pieces in the **Ceramics Gallery** (rooms 136 to 146) are standout items from the Middle East and Asia. The **Dr Susan Weber Gallery** (rooms 133 to 135) celebrates furniture design over the past six centuries.

Temporary Exhibitions

The V&A's temporary exhibitions – covering anything from David Bowie retrospectives to car design, special materials and trends – are compelling and fun (note admission fees apply). Also look out for talks, workshops and events (and one of the best museum shops around).

V&A Tours

Free one-hour guided introductory tours leave the main reception area every day at 10.30am, 12.30pm, 1.30pm and 3.30pm. Check the website for details of other, more specific, tours.

The Exhibition Road Building Project

The Exhibition Road Building Project opened a magnificent new entrance – via the 19th-century screen designed by Sir Aston Webb – leading to the new Sackler Courtyard, as well as the subterranean **Sainsbury Gallery**, a vast new venue for temporary exhibitions.

V&A Through the Ages

The V&A opened in 1852 on the back of the runaway success of the Great Exhibition of 1851 and Prince Albert's enthusiasm for the arts. Its aims were to make art available to all, and to effect 'improvement of public taste in design'. It began with objects first collected by the Government School of Design in the 1830s and '40s and £5000 worth of purchases from the Great Exhibition profits.

Early Expansion

The Museum of Manufactures, as it was then known, moved its eclectic mix of designs and innovations to a collection of semi-permanent buildings in South Kensington in 1857. An expansion brought more ad hoc structures, and in 1890 the museum's board launched a competition to design the museum's new facade on Cromwell Rd and to bring harmony to its architectural hotchpotch. Young architect Aston Webb (who went on to design the facade of Buckingham Palace) won, and Queen Victoria laid the foundation stone in May 1899. The occasion marked a name change, with the Victoria & Albert Museum the new moniker.

Scrapping Admission Charges

When militant suffragettes threatened to damage exhibits at public museums in 1913, the V&A considered denying women entry to the museum, but instead opted for scrapping admission charges to the museum to boost visitor numbers and so help protect the V&A's collection.

V&A in the Wars

The V&A remained open during both world wars. When WWI broke out, several of French sculptor Auguste Rodin's works were on loan at the V&A and the hostilities prevented their return to France. Rodin was so moved by the solidarity of English and French troops that he donated the pieces to the museum. During WWII the museum was hit repeatedly by German bombs (a commemorative inscription remains on Cromwell Rd). Much of the collection had been evacuated (or, as with Raphael's cartoons, bricked in), so damage was minimal.

Top Experience 📷

Explore Nature at the Natural History Museum

This colossal landmark is infused with the irrepressible Victorian spirit of collecting, cataloguing and interpreting the natural world. The main museum building, designed by Alfred Waterhouse in blue- and sand-coloured brick and terracotta, is as much a reason to visit as the world-famous collection within. Kids are the number-one fans, but adults also are enamoured of the exhibits.

◎ MAP P154, D5

www.nhm.ac.uk

Cromwell Rd, SW7

admission free

🕙 10am-5.50pm

👫

Ⓤ South Kensington

Architecture

Be sure to admire the astonishing architecture of Alfred Waterhouse. With carved pillars, animal bas-reliefs, sculptures of plants and beasts, leaded windows and sublime arches, the museum is a work of art and a labour of love.

Hintze Hall

When entering the museum's grand main entrance, this impressive central hall resembles a cathedral nave – fittingly, as it was built in a time when natural sciences were challenging Christian orthodoxy. Naturalist, first superintendent of the museum, and coiner of the word 'dinosaur' Richard Owen celebrated the building as a 'cathedral to nature'.

After 81 years in the Mammals Hall, the blue whale skeleton – Hope – was relocated to Hintze Hall, with the famous cast of a diplodocus skeleton (nicknamed Dippy) making way for the colossal marine mammal. The transfer itself was a mammoth and painstaking engineering project: disassembling and preparing 4.5-tonnes of bones for reconstruction in a dramatic diving posture that greets museum visitors.

Green Zone

While children love the Blue Zone, adults may prefer the Green Zone, especially the Treasures in the **Cadogan Gallery** (1st floor), which houses the museum's most prized possessions, each with a unique history. Exhibits include a chunk of moon rock, an emperor penguin egg collected by Captain Scott's expedition and a first edition of Charles Darwin's *On the Origin of Species*. Equally rare and exceptional are the gems and rocks held in the **Vault**, including a Martian meteorite and the largest emerald ever found. Pause to marvel at the trunk section of a 1300-year-old giant sequoia tree on the 2nd floor: its size is mind-boggling.

★ Top Tips

◦ Take an after-hours museum tour to enjoy an almost empty museum.

◦ Arrive as soon as it opens on weekends or after 2pm weekdays (when school groups have left).

◦ If you arrive early, head to the Dinosaur Gallery first, before it is inundated with visitors.

◦ Avoid Cromwell Rd queues; aim for the Exhibition Rd entrance instead. Ticket holders to ticketed exhibitions get priority access, beating queues.

◦ Download the visitor app for details on highlights and exhibitions.

✖ Take a Break

The museum has several decent cafes for refuelling.

For a pint and tasty pub grub in a classic London mews, head to the **Queen's Arms** (www.thequeens armskensington.co.uk; 30 Queen's Gate Mews, SW7; ⊘noon-11pm; Ⓤ Gloucester Rd).

Back on the ground floor, the superb **Creepy Crawlies Gallery** delves into insect life and whether they're our friends or foes (turns out they're both).

Blue Zone

Undoubtedly the museum's star attraction, the **Dinosaurs Gallery** takes you on an impressive walkway, past a dromaeosaurus (a small and agile meat eater) before reaching a roaring animatronic T-rex and then winding its way through skeletons, fossils, casts and other absorbing dinosaur displays.

Another highlight of this zone is the **Mammals Gallery**, with extensive displays on both living and extinct warm-blooded animals, including the giant, wombat-related diprotodon, the largest marsupial ever to live until it was wiped out around 25,000 years ago. Lest we forget we are part of the animal kingdom, the museum has dedicated a gallery to **Human Biology**, where you'll be able to understand more about what makes us tick (senses, hormones, our brain...).

Red Zone

This zone explores the ever-changing nature of our planet and the forces shaping it. The earthquake simulator (in the **Volcanoes and Earthquakes Gallery**), which recreates the 1995 earthquake in Kobe, Japan (of which you can see footage), is a favourite, as is the **From the Beginning Gallery**, which retraces Earth's history.

In **Earth's Treasury** find out more about our planet's mineral

Animatronic T-rex model, Dinosaurs Gallery

riches and their everyday uses: from jewellery to construction and electronics. Visitors can trace the evolution of our species in the **Human Evolution Gallery**, including an engrossing model of the face of Britain's oldest, almost complete *Homo sapiens* skeleton: Cheddar Man, who lived around 10,000 years ago.

Access to most of the Red Zone galleries is via **Earth Hall** and an escalator that disappears into a huge metal sculpture of the Earth. Sophie the stegosaurus, at the base, is the world's most complete stegosaurus.

Orange Zone

The **Darwin Centre** is the beating heart of the museum. The top two floors of the amazing 'cocoon' building are dedicated to explaining the museum's research – windows even allow you to see the researchers at work. To find out more, pop into the **Attenborough studio** for one of the weekly talks with museum scientists. The studio also shows films throughout the day.

Wildlife Garden

Due to be hugely expanded, this slice of English countryside in SW7 encompasses a range of British lowland habitats, including a meadow with farm gates, a

Exhibitions

The museum hosts regular exhibitions (admission fees apply), some of them on a recurrent basis. A major fixture is autumn's **Wildlife Photographer of the Year** (adult/child £13.95/8.25, family £29-39.50; ☉Oct-Dec), with show-stopping images. See the website for details of other exhibitions.

bee tree where a colony of honey bees fills the air, and a pond. Late summer sees the arrival of greyface Dartmoor sheep. Ornithologists can look out for moorhens, wrens and finches.

Museum Shop

As well as the obligatory dinosaur figurines and animal soft toys, the museum's shop has a brilliant collection of children's books about nature, animals and dinosaurs. On the adult side, browse for beautiful jewellery and lovely stationery.

Ice Skating at the Museum

From around Halloween to January, a section of the museum by the East Lawn is transformed into a glittering and popular ice rink, complete with a hot-drinks stall. Book your slot well ahead, browse the museum and skate later.

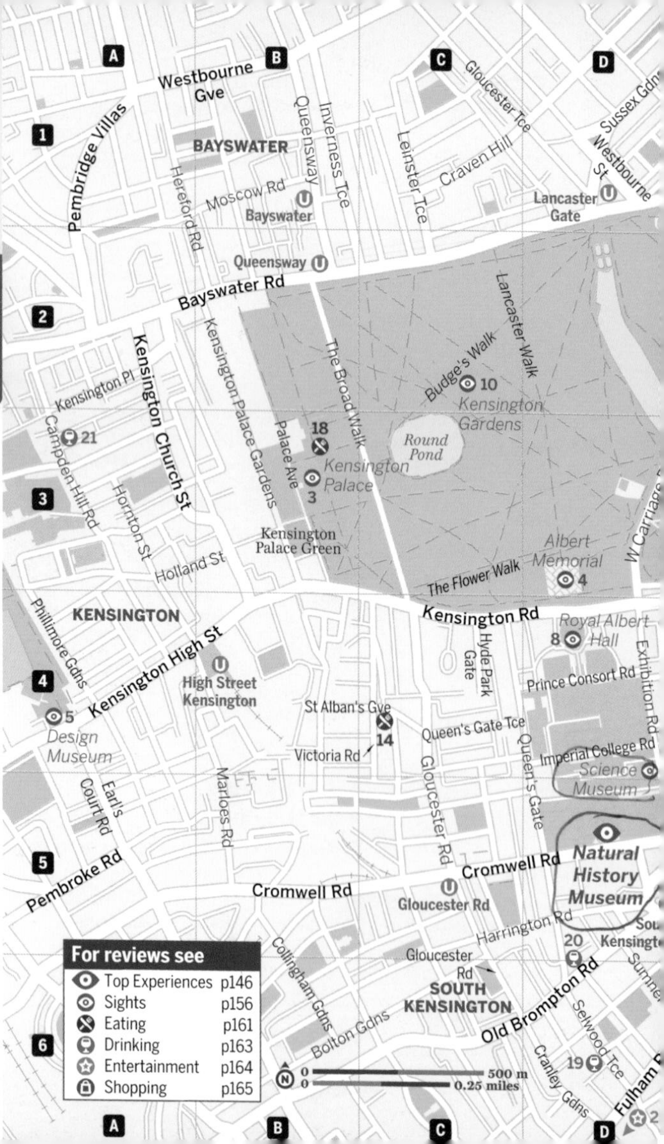

A

1

Pembridge Villas

Westbourne Gve

B

Queensway

Inverness Tce

BAYSWATER

Moscow Rd

Hereford Rd

Bayswater Ⓤ

Queensway Ⓤ

C

Gloucester Tce

Leinster Tce

Craven Hill

Leinster Tce

Lancaster Gate Ⓤ

D

Sussex Gdns

Westbourne St

Lancaster Gate

2

Bayswater Rd

Kensington Pl

Campden Hill Rd

Kensington Church St

Hornton St

Holland St

Kensington Palace Gdns

The Broad Walk

Palace Ave

18 ⊗
Kensington Palace

3 ⊙

Kensington Palace Green

Kensington Palace Green

Budge's Walk

⊙ **10**
Kensington Gardens

Round Pond

W Carriage

Albert Memorial

⊙ **4**

3

Ⓠ **21**

4

Phillimore Gdns

KENSINGTON

Kensington High St

High Street Kensington Ⓤ

Earl's Court Rd

Marloes Rd

St Alban's Gve

⊗ **14**

Victoria Rd

Gloucester Rd

Queen's Gate Tce

Queen's Gate

The Flower Walk

Kensington Rd

Hyde Park Gate

Royal Albert Hall
8 ⊙

Prince Consort Rd

Imperial College Rd

Exhibition Rd

Science Museum
⊙

⊙ **5**
Design Museum

5

Pembroke Rd

Cromwell Rd

Cromwell Rd Ⓤ

Gloucester Rd

Collingham Gdns

Bolton Gdns

Gloucester Rd

Harrington Rd

SOUTH KENSINGTON

Old Brompton Rd

⊙
Natural History Museum

20 Ⓠ Kensingt

Sou

Sumne

Selwood Tce

Cranley Gdns

Fulham

19 ⊕

⊕ 2

6

For reviews see	
⊙ Top Experiences	p146
⊙ Sights	p156
⊗ Eating	p161
⊖ Drinking	p163
⊕ Entertainment	p164
⊕ Shopping	p165

Ⓝ

0 —————— 500 m
0 —————— 0.25 miles

A   **B**   **C**   **D**

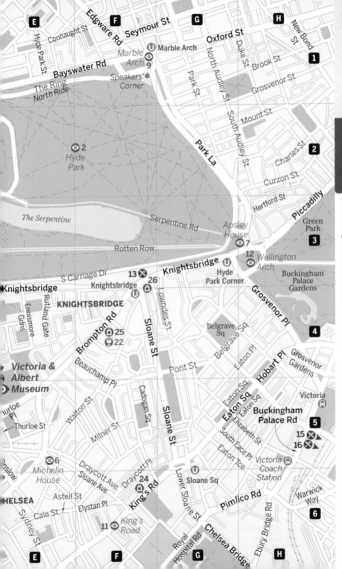

Sights

Science Museum

MUSEUM

1 🔘 MAP P154, D4

This scientifically spellbinding museum will mesmerise adults and children alike, with its interactive and educational exhibits covering everything from early technology to space travel. On the ground floor, a perennial favourite is **Exploring Space**, a gallery featuring genuine rockets and satellites and a full-size replica of the *Eagle*, the lander that took Neil Armstrong and Buzz Aldrin to the moon in 1969. The **Making the Modern World Gallery** next door is a visual feast of locomotives, planes, cars and other revolutionary inventions.

The 2nd-floor displays cover a host of subjects. The **Information Age Gallery** showcases how information and communication technologies – from the telegraph to smartphones – have transformed our lives since the 19th century. Standout displays include the first BBC radio broadcast and a Soviet BESM-6 supercomputer. The **Clockmaker's Museum** is a fascinating collection of timepieces, while **Mathematics: the Winton Gallery**, designed by Zaha Hadid Architects, is a riveting exploration of maths in the real world. The **Medicine Galleries**, opened in 2019, look at the medical world using objects from both the museum's collections and those of Sir Henry Wellcome, pharmacist, philanthropist and collector.

Kensington Palace

The 3rd floor's **Flight Gallery** (free tours 1pm most days) is a favourite place for children, with its gliders, hot-air balloons and aircraft, including the De Havilland Gipsy Moth airplane *Jason I*, which Amy Johnson flew to Australia in 1930. The rest of the floor is all about getting interactive, with the flight-simulation theatre Red Arrows 3D (£5); the Fly 360° flight-simulator capsules (per capsule £12); another simulator, Typhoon Force (£5), replicating a low-level mission aboard a fighter jet; and Space Descent (£7), a virtual-reality experience with (a digital) Tim Peake, British astronaut. Also on the 3rd floor, **Wonderlab: The Equinor Gallery** (adult/child £10/8) explores scientific phenomena in a fun and educational way, with daily shows.

If you've got kids under the age of five, pop down to the basement and the **Garden**, where there's a fun-filled play zone, including a water-play area. (020-7942 4000, 0333 241 4000; www.sciencemuseum.org.uk; Exhibition Rd, SW7; admission free; 10am-6pm, last entry 5.15pm; ; South Kensington)

Hyde Park
PARK

 MAP P154, F2

Hyde Park is central London's largest green space, expropriated from the church in 1536 by Henry VIII and turned into a hunting ground and later a venue for duels, executions and horse racing. The 1851 Great Exhibition was held

Hyde Park's Secret Pet Cemetery

An oddity by Victoria Gate on the north side of Hyde Park, this small boneyard for over one thousand dogs, cats and other pets was founded in 1881, before interring its last furry occupant in 1903. With its midget headstones commemorating legions of affectionately named moggies and mongrels, the cemetery can only be visited on the Hidden Stories of Hyde Park tours (£10) arranged by Royal Parks (www.royalparks.org.uk) on the second Friday of the month; check the website for details.

here, and during WWII the park became an enormous potato field. These days, it's a place to stroll and picnic, boat on the Serpentine lake, or catch a summer concert or outdoor film during the warmer months. (www.royalparks.org.uk/parks/hyde-park; 5am-midnight; Marble Arch, Hyde Park Corner, Knightsbridge or Queensway)

Kensington Palace
PALACE

 MAP P154, B3

Built in 1605, Kensington Palace became the favourite royal residence under William and Mary of Orange in 1689, and remained so until George III became king and relocated to Buckingham Palace. Today, it remains a residence for

Speakers' Corner

Frequented by Karl Marx, Vladimir Lenin, George Orwell and William Morris, **Speakers' Corner** (Map p154, F1; Park Lane; U Marble Arch) in the northeastern corner of Hyde Park is traditionally the spot for oratorical flourishes and soapbox ranting. If you've got something to get off your chest, do so on Sunday, although you'll mainly have fringe dwellers, religious fanatics and hecklers for company.

It's the only place in Britain where demonstrators can assemble without police permission, a concession granted in 1872 after serious riots 17 years before when 150,000 people gathered to demonstrate against the Sunday Trading Bill soon to be debated in Parliament, only to be unexpectedly ambushed by police concealed within Marble Arch. Some historians also link Speakers' Corner with the nearby Tyburn gallows, where condemned criminals might speak to the crowd before being hanged.

high-ranking royals, including the Duke and Duchess of Cambridge (Prince William and his wife Kate). A large part of the palace is open to the public, however, including the King's and Queen's State Apartments. (www.hrp.org.uk/kensington-palace; Kensington Gardens, W8; adult/child £21.50/10.70, cheaper weekdays after 2pm; ⊙10am-6pm, to 4pm Nov-Feb; U High St Kensington)

Albert Memorial   MONUMENT

4 ◉ MAP P154, D3

This splendid Victorian confection on the southern edge of Kensington Gardens is as ostentatious as its subject wasn't. Queen Victoria's humble German husband Albert (1819–61) explicitly insisted he did not want a monument. Ignoring the good prince's wishes, the Lord Mayor instructed George Gilbert Scott to build the 53m-high, gaudy Gothic memorial – the 4.25m-tall gilded statue of the prince, surrounded by 187 figures representing the continents (Asia, Europe, Africa and America), the arts, industry and science, went up in 1876. (☏tours 0300 061 2270; Kensington Gardens; tours £10; ⊙tours 2pm 1st Fri every other month Apr-Oct; U Knightsbridge or Gloucester Rd)

Design Museum   MUSEUM

5 ◉ MAP P154, A4

Relocated from its former Thames location to a stunning new £83-million home by Holland Park, this slick museum is dedicated to design's role in everyday life. Its permanent collection is complemented by a revolving program of special exhibitions, and it's a crucial pit stop for anyone with an eye for recent technology or contemporary aesthetics. Splendidly housed in the refitted former Commonwealth Institute (which opened in 1962), the lavish interior – all smooth Douglas fir and marble – is itself a design triumph. (☏020-3862 5900; www.designmuseum.org; 224-238 Kensington High St, W8; admission free; ⊘10am-6pm, to 8pm or 9pm 1st Fri of month; Ⓤ High St Kensington)

Michelin House   HISTORIC BUILDING

6 ◎ MAP P154, E5

Built for Michelin between 1905 and 1911 by François Espinasse, and completely restored in 1985, the building blurs the stylish line between art nouveau and art deco, both announcing the dawn of the machine age while giving a nod to natural forms. The iconic roly-poly Michelin Man (Bibendum) appears in the exquisite modern stained glass (the originals were removed at the outbreak of WWII and stored in the Michelin factory in Stoke-on-Trent, but subsequently vanished), while the lobby is decorated with tiles illustrating early-20th-century cars. (81 Fulham Rd, SW3; Ⓤ South Kensington)

Apsley House   HISTORIC BUILDING

7 ◎ MAP P154, H3

This stunning house, containing exhibits about the Duke of Wellington, who defeated Napoleon Bonaparte at Waterloo, was once the first building to appear when entering London from the west and was therefore known as 'No 1 London'. Wellington memorabilia, including the Duke's death mask, fills the **basement gallery**, while an astonishing collection

Albert Memorial

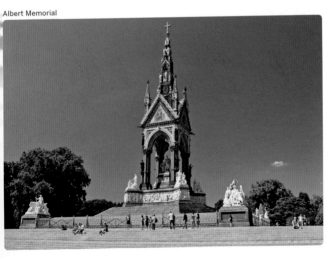

of china and silver, and paintings by Velasquez, Rubens, Van Dyck, Brueghel, Murillo and Goya awaits in the 1st-floor **Waterloo Gallery**. Still one of London's finest buildings, Apsley House was designed by Robert Adam for Baron Apsley in the late 18th century, but later sold to the first Duke of Wellington, who lived here until he died in 1852. (☏ 020-7499 5676; www. english-heritage.org.uk/visit/places/apsley-house; 149 Piccadilly, Hyde Park Corner, W1; adult/child £10.50/6.30, with Wellington Arch £13.60/8.20; ⏱ 11am-5pm Wed-Sun Apr-Oct, 10am-4pm Sat & Sun Nov-Mar; Ⓤ Hyde Park Corner)

Royal Albert Hall

HISTORIC BUILDING

8 ⊙ MAP P154, D4

Built in 1871, thanks in part to the proceeds of the 1851 Great Exhibition organised by Prince Albert, this huge, domed, red-brick amphitheatre, adorned with a frieze of Minton tiles, is Britain's most famous concert venue and home to the BBC's Promenade Concerts (the Proms) every summer. To find out about the hall's intriguing history and royal connections, and to gaze out from the Gallery, book an informative one-hour front-of-house **grand tour** (adult/child £14.25/7.25; ⏱ hourly 9.30am-4.30pm Apr-Oct, 10am-4pm Nov-Mar), operating most days. (☏ 0845 401 5034, box office 020-7589 8212; www. royalalberthall.com; Kensington Gore, SW7; Ⓤ South Kensington)

Marble Arch

MONUMENT

9 ⊙ MAP P154, F1

Designed by John Nash in 1828, this huge white arch was moved here next to Speakers' Corner from its original spot in front of Buckingham Palace in 1851. If you're feeling anarchic, walk through the central portal, a privilege reserved by (unenforced) law for the Royal Family and the ceremonial King's Troop Royal Horse Artillery. (Ⓤ Marble Arch)

Kensington Gardens

PARK

10 ⊙ MAP P154, C2

A delightful collection of manicured lawns, tree-shaded avenues and basins immediately west of Hyde Park, the picturesque expanse of Kensington Gardens is technically part of Kensington Palace (p157), located in the far west of the gardens. The large Round Pond in front of the palace is enjoyable to amble around, and also worth a look are the lovely fountains in the Italian Gardens, believed to be a gift from Prince Albert to Queen Victoria; they are now the venue of a cafe. The Diana, Princess of Wales Memorial Playground, in the northwest corner of the gardens, has some pretty ambitious attractions for children. Next to the playground stands the delightful Elfin Oak, a 900-year-old tree stump carved with elves, gnomes and witches. (☏ 0300 061 2000; www.royalparks.org.uk/parks/kensington-gardens; ⏱ 6am-dusk; Ⓤ Queensway or Lancaster Gate)

King's Road — STREET

11 📍 MAP P154, F6

At the counter-cultural forefront of London fashion during the technicolour '60s and anarchic '70s (Ian Fleming's fictional spy James Bond had a flat in a square off the road), King's Rd today is more a stamping ground for the leisure-class shopping set. The last green-haired Mohawk punks – once tourist sights in themselves – shuffled off sometime in the 1990s. Today it's all Muji, Calvin Klein, Foxtons and a sprinkling of specialist shops; even pet canines are snappily dressed. (U Sloane Sq)

Wellington Arch — MUSEUM

12 📍 MAP P154, H3

Dominating the green space throttled by the Hyde Park Corner roundabout, this imposing neoclassical 1826 Corinthian arch originally faced the Hyde Park Screen, but was shunted here in 1882 for road widening. Once a police station, the arch today has four floors of galleries and temporary exhibition space as well as a permanent display about the history of the arch and a gift shop. The open-air balconies (accessible by lift) afford unforgettable views of Hyde Park, Buckingham Palace and the Mall. (www.english-heritage. org.uk/visit/places/wellington-arch; Hyde Park Corner, W1; adult/child £5.70/3.40, family £14.80, with Apsley House £13.60/8.20, family £35.40; ⏰ 10am-6pm Apr-Sep, to 4pm Nov-Mar; U Hyde Park Corner)

Queen's Life Guard 👍

Catch the Queen's Life Guard (Household Cavalry) departing for Horse Guards Parade at 10.28am (9.28am Sundays) from Hyde Park Barracks for the daily Changing of the Guard, performing a ritual that dates to 1660. They troop via Hyde Park Corner (and under Wellington Arch), Constitution Hill and the Mall. It's not as busy as the Changing of the Guard at Buckingham Palace and you can get closer to the action.

Eating

Dinner by Heston Blumenthal — MODERN BRITISH £££

13 🍴 MAP P154, F3

With two Michelin stars, sumptuously presented Dinner is a gastronomic tour de force, taking diners on a journey through British culinary history (with inventive modern inflections). Dishes carry historical dates to convey context, while the restaurant interior is a design triumph, from the glass-walled kitchen and its overhead clock mechanism to the large windows looking onto the park. (📞 020-7201 3833; www.dinnerbyheston. com; Mandarin Oriental Hyde Park, 66 Knightsbridge, SW1; 3-course set lunch £48, mains £44-52; ⏰ noon-2.15pm & 6-9.30pm Sun-Wed, noon-2.30pm & 6-10pm Thu-Sat; 📶; U Knightsbridge)

Launceston Place

MODERN BRITISH £££

14 ⊗ MAP P154, C4

This exceptionally handsome, superchic Michelin-starred restaurant is almost anonymous on a picture-postcard Kensington street of Edwardian houses. Prepared by London chef Ben Murphy, dishes occupy the acme of gastronomic pleasures and are accompanied by an award-winning wine list. The adventurous will aim for the eight-course tasting menu (£85; vegetarian and vegan versions available). (☏020-7937 6912; www.launcestonplace-restaurant.co.uk; 1a Launceston Pl, W8; mains £22-34, 2-/3-course set lunch £25/29, 2-/3-course set dinner £55-65; ⏱noon-2.30pm Tue-Sat, to 3.30pm Sun, 6-10pm Mon-Sat, 6.30-9pm Sun; ☏; Ⓤ Gloucester Rd or High St Kensington)

A Wong

CHINESE ££

15 ⊗ MAP P154, H5

With its relaxed, appealing vibe and busy open kitchen, Michelin-starred A Wong excels at lunchtime dim sum but also casts its net wide to haul in some very tasty sensations from across China: Shanghai *xiao long bao* dumplings, Shaanxi *roujiamo* (pulled-lamb burger in a bun), Chengdu *doufuhua* (Chengdu 'street tofu'), spicy Sichuan aubergines, Peking duck and more, deliciously

reinterpreted. (☏020-7828 8931; www.awong.co.uk; 70 Wilton Rd, SW1; dim sum per item £2.50, mains £11-35, 'Taste of China' menu £100; ⏱noon-2.30pm & 5.30-10pm Tue-Sat; Ⓤ Victoria)

Pimlico Fresh

CAFE £

16 ⊗ MAP P154, H5

This chirpy two-room cafe will see you right, whether you need breakfast (French toast, bowls of porridge laced with honey, banana, maple syrup or yoghurt), lunch (home-made quiches and soups, 'things' on toast) or just a good old latte and cake. (☏020-7932 0030; 86 Wilton Rd, SW1; mains from £3.50; ⏱7.30am-7.30pm Mon-Fri, 9am-6pm Sat & Sun; Ⓤ Victoria)

V&A Cafe

CAFE £

17 ⊗ MAP P154, E4

There is plenty of hot and cold food to choose from at the V&A Cafe, and the setting is quite astonishingly beautiful: the extraordinarily decorated Morris, Gamble and Poynter Rooms (1868) show Victorian Classic Revival style at its very best – these were the first museums cafes in the world. Plus there's often a piano accompaniment to your tea and cake. (☏020-7581 2159; www.vam.ac.uk/info/va-cafe; Victoria & Albert Museum, Cromwell Rd, SW7; mains £7.45-13.50; ⏱10am-5.10pm Sat-Thu, to 9.15pm Fri; ☏; Ⓤ South Kensington)

V&A Cafe

Kensington Palace Pavilion
BRITISH ££

18 MAP P154, B3

What the Kensington Palace Pavilion lacks in history it makes up for with an excellent menu of breakfasts, light lunches and the standout afternoon tea. The sandwiches, scones and cakes stacked high on their elegant tiers are just the thing for refuelling after a visit to Kensington Palace (p157) itself. To really stick your pinky finger out, go for the Royal Afternoon Tea. (020-3166 6114; www.kensingtonpalacepavilion.co.uk; Kensington Gardens, W8; afternoon tea £34, royal afternoon tea £88; 10am-6pm; ; High St Kensington)

Drinking

Anglesea Arms
PUB

19 MAP P154, D6

Seasoned with age and decades of ale-quaffing patrons (including Charles Dickens, who lived on the same road, and DH Lawrence), this old-school pub boasts considerable character and a strong showing of beers and gins (over two dozen), while the terrace out front swarms with punters in warmer months. Arch-criminal Bruce Reynolds masterminded the 1963 Great Train Robbery over drinks here. (020-7373 7960; www.angleseaarms.com; 15 Selwood Tce, SW7; 11am-11pm Mon-Sat, to 10.30pm Sun; South Kensington)

K Bar

COCKTAIL BAR

20 📷 MAP P154, D5

In a part of town traditionally bereft of choice, the K Bar is a reassuring presence. A hotel bar maybe, but don't let that stop you – the place exudes panache with its leather-panelled and green-marble counter bar, smoothly glinting brass, oak walls, and chandeliers, drawing a cashed-up crowd who enjoy themselves. Cocktails are prepared with as much class as the ambience. (📞020-7589 6300; www.townhouse kensington.com/k-bar; Town House, 109-113 Queen's Gate, SW7; cocktails £10; ⏰4pm-midnight Mon-Thu, to 1am Fri, noon-1am Sat, to 11pm Sun; 📶; Ⓤ South Kensington)

Royal Albert Hall

KAREN MCGAUL/SHUTTERSTOCK ©

Windsor Castle

PUB

21 📷 MAP P154, A3

This classic tavern on the brow of Campden Hill Rd has history, nooks and charm on tap. Along-side a decent beer selection and a solid gastropub-style menu, it has a historic compartmentalised interior, a roaring fire (in winter), a delightful beer garden (in summer) and affable regulars (all seasons). (📞020-7243 8797; www.thewindsor castlekensington.co.uk; 114 Campden Hill Rd, W11; ⏰noon-11pm Mon-Sat, to 10.30pm Sun; 📶; Ⓤ Notting Hill Gate)

Coffee Bar

CAFE

22 📷 MAP P154, F4

When your legs are turning to lead traipsing around Harrods, gravi-tate towards the shop's curvilinear deco-style bar in the Roastery and Bake Hall for some decidedly smooth coffee at the heart of the shopping action. Come evening, it's all coffee negronis and chilled espresso Martinis. Sittings are lim-ited to 45 minutes. (www.harrods. com; Harrods, 87-135 Brompton Rd, SW1; ⏰10am-9pm Mon-Sat, 11.30am-6pm Sun; 📶; Ⓤ Knightsbridge)

Entertainment

Royal Albert Hall

CONCERT VENUE

This splendid Victorian concert hall (see 8 📷 Map p154, D4) hosts classical music, rock and other performances, but is famously the venue for the BBC-sponsored Proms. Booking is possible, but from mid-July to mid-September

Promenaders queue for £5 standing tickets that go on sale one hour before curtain-up. Otherwise, the box office and prepaid-ticket collection counter are through door 12 on the south side of the hall. (☏0845 401 5034, box office 020-7589 8212; www.royalalberthall.com; Kensington Gore, SW7; Ⓤ South Kensington)

606 Club
BLUES, JAZZ

23 ⭐ MAP P154, D6

Named after its old address on the King's Rd, which cast a spell over London's jazz lovers back in the '80s, this choice, tucked-away basement jazz club and restaurant gives centre stage nightly to contemporary British-based jazz musicians. The club can only serve alcohol to nonmembers who are dining, and it is highly advisable to book to get a table. (☏020-7352 5953; www.606club.co.uk; 90 Lots Rd, SW10; from £10; ⊙doors open 7pm Sun-Thu, 8pm Fri & Sat, plus 12.30pm Sun; Ⓤ Imperial Wharf)

Shopping

John Sandoe Books
BOOKS

24 🔒 MAP P154, F6

Steeped in literary charm and a perfect antidote to impersonal book superstores, this three-storey bookshop in an 18th-century premises inhabits its own universe. A treasure trove of literary gems and hidden surprises, it's been in business for over six decades. (☏020-7589 9473; www.johnsandoe.com; 10 Blacklands Tce, SW3; ⊙9.30am-6.30pm Mon-Sat, 11am-5pm Sun; Ⓤ Sloane Sq)

Harrods
DEPARTMENT STORE

25 🔒 MAP P154, F4

Garish and stylish in equal measure, perennially crowded Harrods is an obligatory stop for visitors, from the cash-strapped to the big spenders. The stock is astonishing, as are many of the price tags. Many visitors don't make it past the ground floor where designer bags, myriad scents from the perfume hall and the mouth-watering counters of the food hall provide plenty of entertainment. (☏020-7730 1234; www.harrods.com; 87-135 Brompton Rd, SW1; ⊙10am-9pm Mon-Sat, 11.30am-6pm Sun; Ⓤ Knightsbridge)

Harvey Nichols
DEPARTMENT STORE

26 🔒 MAP P154, F3

At London's temple of high fashion, you'll find Chloé and Balenciaga bags, the city's best denim range, a massive make-up hall with exclusive lines and great jewellery. The food hall and in-house restaurant, Fifth Floor Cafe, are, you guessed it, on the 5th floor. From 11.30am to noon on Sunday, it's browsing time only (big stores can't sell products until noon on Sundays). (☏020-7235 5000; www.harveynichols.com; 109-125 Knightsbridge, SW1; ⊙10am-8pm Mon-Sat, 11.30am-6pm Sun; Ⓤ Knightsbridge)

Walking Tour 🥾

A Saturday in Notting Hill

A Notting Hill Saturday sees the neighbourhood at its busiest and best. Buzzing Portobello Road Market radiates vibrant colour, and excellent restaurants, shops and an absorbing museum make the day an event that embraces market and shop browsing, culinary surprises, book-hunting and a chance to catch a film in a classic picture-house setting.

Getting There

Ⓤ Notting Hill Gate station is on the Circle, District and Central Lines.

Ⓤ Ladbroke Grove station on the Hammersmith & City and Circle Lines is also useful.

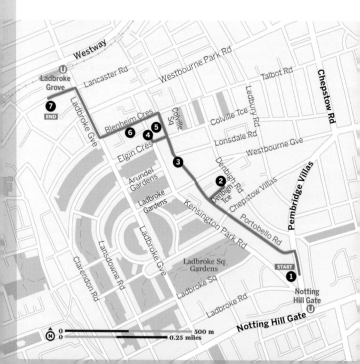

❶ Stock up on Snacks

Close to Notting Hill Gate Tube station and en route to Portobello Market, you can't miss **Arancina** (www.arancina.co.uk; 19 Pembridge Rd, W11; mains £3.30-23; ⏰8am-11pm Mon-Sat, 9am-11pm Sun) with its orange cut-out Fiat 500 in the window. It's a great spot for *arancine* (fried rice balls with fillings), freshly baked pizza, craft beer or a glass of red.

❷ A Splash of Colour

Delve into **Denbigh Terrace** for its row of vibrantly painted terraced houses on the south side of the street, which make for a candy-coloured photo-op, especially if it's sunny.

❸ Browse the Market

Stroll along Portobello Rd until you reach the iconic **Portobello Road Market** (www.portobellomarket.org; Portobello Rd, W10; ⏰9am-6pm Mon-Wed, to 7pm Fri & Sat, to 1pm Thu). The market mixes street food with fruit and veg, antiques, colourful fashion and trinkets.

❹ Book Hunting

Divert left to visit **Lutyens & Rubinstein** (www.lutyensrubinstein.co.uk; 21 Kensington Park Rd, W11; ⏰10am-6pm Mon & Sat, to 6.30pm Tue-Fri, 11am-5pm Sun) bookshop. Its small size pays dividends. Established by a pair of literary agents, it focuses discerningly on 'excellence in writing', as determined by customers and readers.

❺ Catch a Film & a Burger

Wander back to Portobello Rd to the **Electric Cinema** (www.electriccinema.co.uk; 191 Portobello Rd, W11; tickets £17.50-45), one of the UK's oldest cinemas, with luxurious leather armchairs, footstools, sofas and even front-row double beds! Check the fabulous tiled floor interior. When the credits roll, head to **Honest Burgers** (www.honestburgers.co.uk; 189 Portobello Rd, W11; mains £9-14; ⏰11am-11pm Mon-Sat, to 10pm Sun) next door for terrific bites.

❻ Blenheim Crescent

Turn left into Blenheim Cres for a string of browse-worthy shops, including glassware at **Ceramica Blue** (www.ceramicablue.co.uk; 10 Blenheim Cres, W11; ⏰10am-6.30pm Mon-Sat, 11am-5pm Sun), and the **Notting Hill Bookshop** (www.thenottinghillbookshop.co.uk; 13 Blenheim Cres; ⏰9am-7pm Mon-Sat, 10am-6pm Sun), the inspiration behind the shop in Hugh Grant and Julia Roberts' rom-com *Notting Hill*.

❼ Get All Nostalgic

Take a left off Ladbroke Grove to the excellent **Museum of Brands** (www.museumofbrands.com; 111-117 Lancaster Rd, W11; adult/child £9/5, family £24; ⏰10am-6pm Mon-Sat, 11am-5pm Sun), which retraces the history of consumer culture. It'll amuse the kids and make the grown-ups nostalgic over the retro packaging and iconic products from days gone by.

Explore ✦
Regent's Park
& Camden

Regent's Park, Camden Market and Hampstead Heath should top your list for excursions into North London. Camden is a major sight with an intoxicating energy and brilliant nightlife, while Regent's Park is an oasis of calm and sophistication amid the North London buzz. Meanwhile, Hampstead Heath offers you a glorious day out and an insight into how North Londoners spend their weekends.

The Short List

- **Camden Market (p174)** *Soaking up the frantic energy of this legendary market.*

- **Hampstead Heath (p174)** *Enjoying the sweeping views of London from Parliament Hill.*

- **ZSL London Zoo (p175)** *Meeting and communing with furred and feathered friends.*

- **Regent's Park (p175)** *Exploring central London's largest and most elaborate Royal Park.*

- **Madame Tussauds (p175)** *Ogling at idols (and otherwise) at the world's most celebrated waxworks.*

Getting There & Around

Ⓤ For Regent's Park, Baker St (on the Jubilee, Metropolitan, Circle, Hammersmith & City and Bakerloo Lines) is most useful. The best stations for Camden are Camden Town and Chalk Farm on the Northern Line. Hampstead is also on the Northern Line.

Neighbourhood Map on p172

Camden Market (p174) GIORGIO ROSSI/SHUTTERSTOCK ©

Walking Tour 🚶

Highlights of North London

Part of the appeal of North London is that it's a great area to just wander – in parks and markets and along canals. This itinerary takes in some of the most atmospheric spots, as well as the big-hitting sights. If you can, stay into the evening to enjoy Camden's fantastic live-music scene.

Walk Facts

Start Madame Tussauds;
Ⓤ Baker St

End Lock Tavern;
Ⓤ Chalk Farm

Length 2.5 miles;
2½ hours

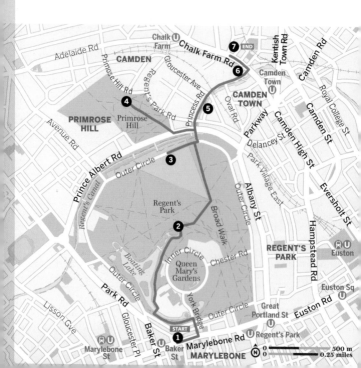

❶ Madame Tussauds

Make sure you pack your selfie stick for a chance to pose with your idols at this waxwork museum (p175) – there are plenty of personalities to ogle and (maybe) admire, from past and current political figures to sportspeople, actors, singers and movie characters.

❷ Regent's Park

Walk along Marylebone Rd, turn left onto York Gate and head into Regent's Park (p175) over York Bridge. Follow the shores of the boating lake to explore the most scenic parts of the park before heading east and joining the Broad Walk, the park's main avenue.

❸ London Zoo

Explore London's famous zoo (p175), where enclosures have been developed to be as close to the animals' original habitats as possible – among the highlights are Land of the Lions, Gorilla Kingdom, In with the Lemurs, Night Life and Penguin Beach.

❹ Views from Primrose Hill

Cross Regent's Canal and make your way towards the top of Primrose Hill for fantastic views of London's skyline. The park is very popular with picnickers and families at the weekend.

❺ Regent's Canal

Head back down Primrose Hill and join the picturesque Regent's Canal towpath for an easy stroll towards Camden. The path is lined with residential narrow boats and old warehouses converted into modern flats. Leave the towpath when you reach Camden Lock and its market.

❻ Camden Market

Browse the bags, clothes, jewellery and arts and crafts stalls of Camden's famous market. There are two main market areas, but they both sell more or less the same things. Camden Lock Market (p179) is the original; push into Stables Market (p179) for more rummaging.

❼ Restorative Drink

Settle in for a well-earned drink at the Lock Tavern (p177), and if the weather is good, sit on the roof terrace and watch the world go by. Check out what's on in the evening, too, as the pub hosts regular bands and DJs.

✕ Take a Break

Camden Lock Market is packed full of takeaway stalls in the West Yard (p176), offering a dazzling array of world cuisines – from French crêpes to Chinese, Argentine grills and sushi, it's all there. Those with a sweet tooth should make a beeline for Chin Chin Labs (p176) and its liquid-nitrogen ice creams.

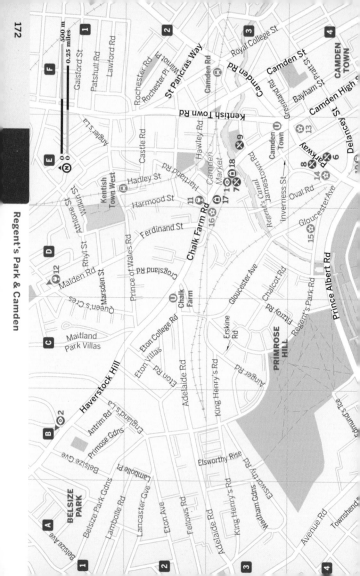

Regent's Park & Camden

500 m
0.25 miles

BELSIZE PARK

Haverstock Hill

Belsize Ave
Belsize Park Gdns
Lambolle Rd
Lancaster Gve
Eton Ave
Fellows Rd
Adelaide Rd
King Henry's Rd
King Henry's Rd
Wadham Gdns

Belsize Gve
Lambolle Pl
Primrose Gdns
Antrim Rd
England's La
Elsworthy Rise
Elsworthy Rd

PRIMROSE HILL

Maitland Park Villas
Queen's Cres
Malden Rd
Marsden St
Rhyl St
Athlone St
Wilkin St

Prince of Wales' Rd
Crogsland Rd
Ferdinand St
Chalk Farm Rd
Harmood St
Hadley St
Castle Rd
Hartland Rd

Eton College Rd
Eton Villas
Eton Rd
Adelaide Rd
Erskine Rd
Anger Rd

Chalk Farm

Gloucester Ave
Chalcot Rd
Fitzroy Rd
Regent's Park Rd
Gloucester Ave

Prince Albert Rd

Kentish Town West
Kentish Town Rd
Camden Market
Camden High St
Camden Town
CAMDEN TOWN

St Pancras Way
Rochester Rd
Rochester Pl
Wilmot Pl
Camden Rd
Royal College St
Camden St
Greenland Rd
Bayham St
Pratt St
Delancey

Camden Rd
Hawley Rd
Hawley St
Camden St
Regent's Canal
Jamestown Rd
Inverness St
Oval Rd
Gloucester Ave

Parkway

Galsford St
Patshull Rd
Lawford Rd

12
2
11
16
9
18
1
17
7
13
8
14
6
15

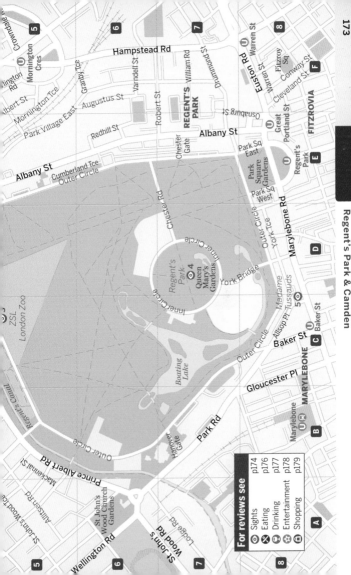

Regent's Park & Camden

Crownd[ale]

5

U Mornington
Cres

Mornington
Rd

Albert St

Mornington Tce

Park Village East

Augustus St

Granby Tce

Varndell St

Robert St

Redhill St

6

Hampstead Rd

REGENT'S
PARK

William Rd

Drummond St

7

Euston Rd

U Warren St

Warren St

Onsburg St

Fitzroy
Sq

Cleveland St

Conway St

8

F

Albany St

Great
Portland St

FITZROVIA

E

Albany St

Cumberland Tce
Outer Circle

Chester
Gate

Albany St

Park Square
East

Park
Square
Gardens

U Regent's
Park

Park Sq
West

Outer Circle

York Tce

Marylebone Rd

D

Chester Rd

Inner Circle

Regent's
Park

4

Queen
Mary's
Gardens

Madame
Tussauds

Allsop Pl

York Bridge

York Bridge

5

ZSL
London Zoo

Inner Circle

Boating
Lake

Outer Circle

Baker St

U Baker St

C

Baker St

Outer Circle

Gloucester Pl

MARYLEBONE

Regent's Canal

Hanover
Gate

Park Rd

Marylebone

U R

Marylebone

B

Prince Albert Rd

Mackennal St

Outer Circle

St John's
Wood Church
Gardens

St John's Wood Tce

Allitsen Rd

5

Wellington Rd

St John's
Wood Rd

Lodge Rd

6

7

A

8

Sights

Camden Market

MARKET

1 ◎ MAP P172, E3

Although it stopped being cutting-edge several thousand cheap leather jackets ago, Camden Market attracts millions of visitors each year and is one of London's most popular attractions. What started out as a collection of attractive craft stalls beside Camden Lock on the Regent's Canal now extends most of the way from Camden Town Tube station to Chalk Farm Tube station. You'll find a bit of everything: clothes, bags, jewellery, candles, incense and myriad decorative titbits. (www.camdenmarket. com; Camden High St, NW1; ◷10am-late; Ⓤ Camden Town or Chalk Farm)

Hampstead Heath

PARK

2 ◎ MAP P172, B1

Sprawling Hampstead Heath, with its rolling woodlands and meadows, feels a million miles away – despite being about 3.5 miles from Trafalgar Sq. It covers 320 hectares, most of it woods, hills and meadows, and is home to about 180 bird species, 25 species of butterflies, grass snakes, bats and a rich array of flora. It's a wonderful place for a ramble, especially to the top of Parliament Hill, which offers expansive views across flat-as-a-pancake London. Note that signage is limited, but getting a little lost is part of the experience. (www.cityoflondon.gov.uk/things-to-do/green-spaces/hampstead-heath; Ⓤ Hampstead Heath or Gospel Oak)

Regent's Canal (p177)

ZSL London Zoo ZOO

3 MAP P172, C5

Opened in 1828, London Zoo is the oldest in the world. The emphasis nowadays is firmly on conservation, breeding and education, with fewer animals and bigger enclosures. Highlights include Land of the Lions, Gorilla Kingdom, the walk-through In with the Lemurs, Night Life and Penguin Beach. There are regular feeding sessions and talks; various experiences are available, such as Keeper for a Day; and you can even spend the night in one of nine Gir Lion Lodge cabins. (☏0344-225 1826; www. zsl.org/zsl-london-zoo; Outer Circle, Regent's Park, NW1; adult £25-32.50; child £16-20.50; ⊙10am-6pm Apr-Aug, to 5pm mid-Feb–Mar, Sep & Oct, to 4pm Nov–mid-Feb; 👪; 🚌88 or 274)

Regent's Park PARK

4 MAP P172, D7

The largest and most elaborate of central London's many Royal Parks, Regent's Park is one of the capital's loveliest green spaces. Among its many attractions are London Zoo, Regent's Canal, an ornamental lake, and sports pitches where locals meet to play football, rugby and volleyball. Queen Mary's Gardens, towards the south of the park, are particularly pretty. Performances take place here in an **open-air theatre** (☏0333 400 3562; www.openairtheatre.org) during summer. (www.royalparks.org.uk/ parks/the-regents-park; ⊙5am-dusk; Ⓤ Regent's Park or Baker St)

North London Neighbourhoods ⓘ

North London is a collection of small neighbourhoods, originally ancient villages that were slowly drawn into London's orbit as the metropolis expanded. It's a very green area, home to some of the largest and most beautiful park spaces in the city. Sights are pretty scattered in the northern half of the area, where you'll need some leg power to explore hilly Hampstead. King's Cross, however, is a lot more compact. A walk along Regent's Canal will link Regent's Park, Camden and King's Cross.

Madame Tussauds MUSEUM

5 MAP P172, C8

It may be kitschy and pricey, but Madame Tussauds makes for a fun-filled day. There are photo ops with your dream celebrity (be it Daniel Craig, Lady Gaga, Benedict Cumberbatch or Audrey Hepburn), the Bollywood gathering (sparring studs Hrithik Roshan and Salman Khan) and the Royal Appointment (the Queen, Harry and Meghan, William and Kate). Book online for much cheaper rates and check the website for seasonal opening hours. (☏0870 400 3000; www. madame-tussauds.com/london; Marylebone Rd, NW1; adult/child £35/30; ⊙10am-6pm; Ⓤ Baker St)

Eating

Hook Camden Town

FISH & CHIPS £

6 MAP P172, E4

In addition to working entirely with sustainable small fisheries and local suppliers, Hook makes all its sauces on-site and wraps its fish in recycled materials, supplying diners with extraordinarily fine-tasting morsels. Totally fresh, the fish arrives in panko breadcrumbs or tempura batter, with seaweed salted chips. Wash it down with craft beer, wines and cocktails. There's also a great kids' menu.

Sauces go beyond the usual suspects, and range from tartare and garlic truffle to chipotle and lemon Cajun. (☑020-7482 0475; www.hookrestaurants.com; 63-65 Parkway, NW1; mains £11-17; ◷noon-3pm & 5.30-9pm Mon, to 10pm Tue-Thu, to 10.30pm Fri & Sat, to 9pm Sun; ⛹; ⓤCamden Town)

Camden Market Snacks

🍽

There are dozens of food stalls at the West Yard of Camden Lock Market (p179), where you can find virtually every type of cuisine, from French to Argentinian, Japanese and Caribbean. Quality varies but is generally pretty good and affordable, and you can eat on the large communal tables or down by the canal.

Chin Chin Labs

ICE CREAM £

7 MAP P172, E3

This is food chemistry at its absolute best. Chefs prepare the ice-cream mixture and freeze it on the spot by adding liquid nitrogen. Flavours change regularly and match the seasons (tonka bean, Valrhona chocolate, burnt-butter caramel or pandan leaf, for instance). The dozen toppings and sauces are equally creative. Try the ice-cream sandwich (£5.65): ice cream wedged inside gorgeous brownies or cookies. (☑07885 604284; www.chinchinlabs.com; 49-50 Camden Lock Pl, NW1; ice cream from £5; ◷noon-7pm; ⓤCamden Town)

Namaaste Kitchen

INDIAN ££

8 MAP P172, E4

Although everything is of a high standard, if there's one thing you should try at Namaaste, it's the kebab platter: the meat and fish coming off the kitchen grill are beautifully tender and incredibly flavoursome. The bread basket is another hit, with specialities such as spiced *missi roti* (flatbread of wholewheat and gram flour and spices). (☑020-7485 5977; www.namaastekitchen.co.uk; 64 Parkway, NW1; mains £10-23; ◷noon-11.30pm Mon-Sat, to 11pm Sun; ⛹; ⓤCamden Town)

Poppies

FISH & CHIPS ££

9 MAP P172, E3

The largest of the three branches of this high-viz chippy serves reliable

Walking along Regent's Canal

The canals that were once a trade lifeline for the capital have now become a favourite escape for Londoners, providing a quiet walk away from traffic and crowds. You can walk from Little Venice to Camden in less than an hour; on the way, you'll pass Regent's Park, London Zoo, Primrose Hill, beautiful villas designed by architect John Nash and redevelopments of old industrial buildings into trendy blocks of flats. Allow 15 to 20 minutes between Camden and Regent's Park, and 25 to 30 minutes between Regent's Park and Little Venice. There are plenty of exits and signposts along the way.

fish (choose from a half dozen types) and chips to up to 110 diners over two levels just opposite the major magnet that is Camden Market. Great decor, too, with reclaimed (or repurposed) 1940s fixtures and fittings throughout. (☎020-7267 0440; www.poppiesfishandchips.co.uk; 30 Hawley Cres, NW1; mains £7-22; ⏱11am-11pm Sun-Thu, to midnight Sat & Sun; ⓤCamden Town)

Drinking

Edinboro Castle   PUB

10 🚇 MAP P172, E4

Large and relaxed, the Edinboro offers a fun atmosphere, a fine bar and a full menu. The highlight, however, is the huge beer garden, complete with warm-weather barbecues and decorated with coloured lights on long summer evenings. Patio heaters appear in winter. (☎020-7255 9651; www.edinborocastlepub.co.uk; 57 Mornington Tce, NW1; ⏱noon-11pm Mon-Sat, to 10.30pm Sun; 🛜; ⓤCamden Town)

Lock Tavern   PUB

11 🚇 MAP P172, E2

A Camden institution, the black-clad Lock Tavern rocks: it's cosy inside, and it has a rear beer garden and a great roof terrace from where you can watch the market throngs. Beer is plentiful here and the pub proffers a prolific roll call of guest bands and well-known DJs at weekends to rev things up. Dancing is encouraged. Entry is always free. (☎020-7482 7163; www.lock-tavern.com; 35 Chalk Farm Rd, NW1; ⏱noon-midnight Sun-Thu, to 1am Fri & Sat; ⓤChalk Farm)

Garden Gate   PUB

12 🚇 MAP P172, D1

At the bottom of Hampstead Heath hides this gem housed in a 19th-century cottage with a gorgeous beer garden. The interior is wonderfully cosy, with dark-wood tables, upholstered chairs and an assortment of distressed sofas. It serves Pimm's and lemonade in summer and mulled wine in winter, both ideal after a long walk. The food (mains £11 to £20) is good, too. (☏020-7435 4938; www.thegardengatehampstead.co.uk; 14 South End Rd, NW3; ⏱noon-11pm Mon-Thu, to midnight Fri, 10am-midnight Sat, noon-10.30pm Sun; ⏺🐾; Ⓤ Hampstead Heath)

Entertainment

Jazz Cafe
LIVE MUSIC

13 ⭐ MAP P172, E4

The name would have you think jazz is the main staple, but it's only a small slice of what's on offer here. The intimate club-like space also serves up funk, hip-hop, R&B, soul and rare groove, with big-name acts regularly playing daily at 7pm. Friday (world music) and Saturday (soul, disco and house) club nights start at 10.30pm. (☏020-7485 6834; www.thejazzcafelondon.com; 5 Parkway, NW1; ⏱7-11pm Sun-Thu, to 3am Fri & Sat; Ⓤ Camden Town)

Green Note
LIVE MUSIC

14 ⭐ MAP P172, E4

Camden may be the home of punk but it also has the Green Note: one of the best places in London to see live folk and world music, with gigs every night of the week. The setting is intimate: a tiny bare-brick room with mics set up in a corner, backdropped by red curtains. Most tickets are under £10 (£12 at the door). (☏020-7485 9899; www.greennote.co.uk; 106 Parkway, NW1; ⏱7-11pm Sun-Thu, to midnight Fri & Sat; Ⓤ Camden Town)

Stables Market

Cecil Sharp House

TRADITIONAL MUSIC

5 ⭐ MAP P172, D4

Home to the English Folk Dance and Song Society, this institute keeps all manner of folk traditions alive. Performances and classes range from traditional British music and ceilidh dances to bell-jingling Morris dancing and clog-stamping, all held in its mural-covered Kennedy Hall. The dance classes are oodles of fun and there's a real community vibe. (📞020-7485 2206; www.cecilsharp house.org; 2 Regent's Park Rd, NW1; ⏰9am-11pm; Ⓤ Camden Town)

FEST Camden

LIVE MUSIC

16 ⭐ MAP P172, D3

Tucked away in what used to be the horse hospital in Camden Stables Market, this space now hosts a diverse range of events, from cinema nights to club nights and from cabaret to comedy. (📞020-7428 4922; www.festcamden.com; Chalk Farm Rd, NW1; ⏰noon-11pm Sun-Wed, to 2.30am Thu-Sat; Ⓤ Chalk Farm)

Shopping

Stables Market

MARKET

17 🔒 MAP P172, E3

Connected to the Camden Lock Market, the Stables overflows with antiques, Asian artefacts, rugs, retro furniture and street clothing. As the name suggests, this is where up to 800 horses (who worked hauling barges on Regent's

North London Sounds

North London is the home of indie rock, and many a famous band started out playing in the area's grungy bars. Indeed, Camden High St has become a rock music Walk of Fame, with the unveiling of a granite plaque dedicated to the Who, the first of a planned 400. You can be sure to find live music of some kind every night of the week. A number of venues are multipurpose, with gigs in the first part of the evening (generally around 7pm or 8pm), followed by club nights beginning around midnight.

Canal) were housed. One potential draw here beyond shopping is the bronze statue of Amy Winehouse (1983–2011), the late and much missed singer-songwriter who lived in the neighbourhood. (www. camdenmarket.com; Chalk Farm Rd, NW1; ⏰10am-late; Ⓤ Chalk Farm)

Camden Lock Market

MARKET

18 🔒 MAP P172, E3

Right next to the canal lock, this section of Camden Market is the place to go for diverse food stalls in the West Yard (p176), as well as for several nice bars with views of the canal. There are also shops selling crafts, ceramics and clothes. (www.camdenmarket.com; Camden Lock Pl, NW1; ⏰10am-late; Ⓤ Camden Town)

Walking Tour 🚶

Walking on Hampstead Heath

Sprawling Hampstead Heath, with its rolling woodlands and meadows, feels a million miles away from central London. Covering 320 hectares, it's home to about 180 bird species, a rich mix of flora and expansive views from the top of Parliament Hill. The heath is particularly busy with families and dog walkers at weekends, and picnicking friends on sunny days.

Getting There

Ⓤ Hampstead station on the Northern Line. For Highgate Cemetery, get off at Archway (Bank branch of the Northern Line).

🚆 Hampstead Heath and Gospel Oak on the Overground.

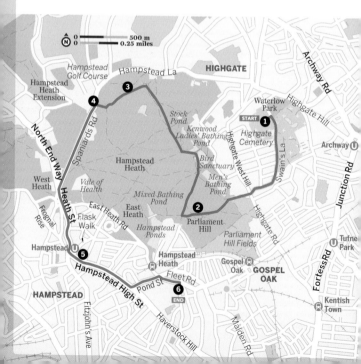

❶ Highgate Cemetery

Final resting place of Karl Marx, George Eliot and Russian secret-service agent Alexander Litvinenko, **Highgate Cemetery** (www.highgatecemetery.org; Swain's Lane, N6; adult/child £4/free; ☺10am-5pm Mar-Oct, to 4pm Nov-Feb) is divided into East and West. To visit the atmospheric West Cemetery, you must take a tour.

❷ Parliament Hill

Head down Swain's Lane to the Highgate West Hill roundabout and climb to Parliament Hill for grand views south over town. Londoners adore picnicking here – choose your spot and feast on the superb vistas. If the weather is warm, swim at the **Hampstead Heath Ponds** (adult/child £4/1; ☺from 7am, closing times vary with season), most of which are open year-round and lifeguard-supervised.

❸ Visit Kenwood House

Traverse the heath to the magnificent neoclassical 18th-century **Kenwood House** (www.english-heritage.org.uk/visit/places/kenwood; Hampstead Lane, NW3; admission free; ☺10am-4pm) in a glorious sweep of perfectly landscaped gardens leading down to a picturesque pond. The house contains a magnificent collection of art, including paintings by Rembrandt, Constable, Turner, Gainsborough and Vermeer. Seek out the Henry Moore and Barbara Hepworth sculptures in the grounds, too.

❹ Rest at the Spaniard's Inn

At the heath's edge is this marvellous 1585 tavern, where Romantic poets Keats and Byron and artist Sir Joshua Reynolds all paused for a tipple. Once a toll house, the **Spaniard's Inn** (www.thespaniardshampstead.co.uk; Spaniards Rd, NW3; ☺noon-11pm Mon-Sat, to 10.30 Sun) has kept its historic charm – wood panelling, jumbled interior and hearty welcome – and is hugely popular with dog walkers, families and other parkgoers on weekends.

❺ Explore Hampstead

Take bus 210 to the Jack Straw's Castle stop and walk down to the historic neighbourhood of Hampstead, a delightful corner of London. Loved by artists in the interwar years, it has retained a bohemian feel, with sumptuous houses, leafy streets and lovely boutiques. Try **Exclusivo** (2 Flask Walk, NW3; ☺12.30-6pm) for top-quality, second-hand designer garments.

❻ Dinner at the Stag

Finish with a stroll down to the **Stag** (www.thestagnw3.com; 67 Fleet Rd, NW3; mains £9-17.50; ☺noon-11pm Mon-Thu, to midnight Fri & Sat, to 10.30 Sun), a fine gastropub where you'll be rewarded with delicious British fare. The beef-and-ale pie is one of a kind, and the desserts are stellar. The wine and beer selection will ensure you're in no rush to go home.

Explore ⊚
Shoreditch & the East End

These historic neighbourhoods contain a few significant sights, mainly around Clerkenwell and Spitalfields, but are best known for culture and nightlife. Shoreditch and Hoxton long ago replaced Soho and Camden as the best places to party, with a mix of great pubs, bars and small clubs. These are some of London's most colourful neighbourhoods, punctuated by street art and vintage stores.

The Short List

○ **Shoreditch nightlife (p189)** *Donning your hippest outfit and heading to Shoreditch for cocktails.*

○ **Super Market Sunday (p184)** *Crawling the markets with the multicultural masses along Columbia Rd and Brick Lane.*

○ **Old Spitalfields Market (p191)** *Searching out treasure (and trash!) and stopping for a bite to eat.*

○ **Dennis Severs' House (p187)** *Entering the quirky time capsule that is this 18th-century Huguenot abode.*

○ **Breddos Tacos (p188)** *Rolling up your sleeves and getting set to sample some of London's best tacos.*

Getting There & Around

U Liverpool St is the closest stop to Spitalfields. Old St is the best stop for the western edge of Hoxton and Shoreditch.

R Shoreditch High St and Hoxton are the closest stations to Spitalfields and the eastern parts of Shoreditch and Hoxton.

🚌 Useful buses include the 8, 55 and 242.

Neighbourhood Map on p186

Walking Tour 🚶

A Sunday in the East End

The East End has a colourful and multicultural history. Waves of migrants (French Protestant, Jewish, Bangladeshi) have left their mark on the area, which, added to the Cockney heritage and the 21st-century hipster phenomenon, has created an incredibly vibrant neighbourhood. It's best appreciated on Sundays, when the area's markets are in full swing.

Walk Facts

Start Columbia Road Flower Market; Ⓤ Hoxton

End Yuu Kitchen; Ⓤ Aldgate East

Length 1.2km, three to four hours

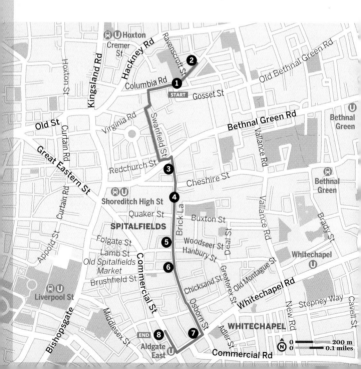

❶ Columbia Road Flower Market

This weekly **market** (www.columbia road.info; Columbia Rd, E2; ⏰8am-3pm Sun) sells an amazing array of flowers and plants. It's lots of fun and the best place to hear proper Cockney barrow-boy banter. It gets packed, so go early.

❷ Pub Break

Escape the crush in the wood-lined confines of the **Royal Oak** (☏020-7729 2220; www.royaloaklondon.com; 73 Columbia Rd, E2; ⏰6.30-10pm Mon-Fri, noon-10pm Sat, noon-4pm & 5-9pm Sun; 🍴), a lovely old East End pub with a little garden out the back.

❸ Grab a Bagel

Brick Lane was once the centre of the Jewish East End. Much of the Jewish community has moved to other areas, but the no-frills Beigel Bake (p189) still does a roaring trade in dirt-cheap homemade bagels.

❹ Brick Lane Market

This street is best known for its huge Sunday **market** (www.visit bricklane.org; Brick Lane, E1; ⏰10am-5pm Sun). You'll find anything from vintage to bric-a-brac, cheap fashion and food stalls.

❺ Old Truman Brewery

Founded in the 17th century and the largest brewery in the world by the 1850s, Truman's buildings and yards straddle both sides of Brick Lane. The complex now hosts edgy markets, including the funky **Sunday Upmarket** (www.sunday upmarket.co.uk; Old Truman Brewery, 91 Brick Lane, E1; ⏰11am-5.30pm Sat, 10am-6pm Sun), featuring young fashion designers.

❻ Brick Lane Great Mosque

No building better symbolises the waves of immigration in this area: the 1743 Huguenot New French Church was converted to a Methodist chapel in 1819, transformed into the Great Synagogue for Jewish refugees in 1898, before becoming the Great Mosque in 1976.

❼ Whitechapel Gallery

This ground-breaking **gallery** (www.whitechapelgallery.org; 77-82 Whitechapel High St, E1; admission free; ⏰11am-6pm Tue, Wed & Fri-Sun, to 9pm Thu) has no permanent collection, but hosts contemporary art exhibitions. It made its name by staging exhibitions by both established and emerging artists, including the first UK shows by Pablo Picasso and Frida Khalo.

❽ Yuu Kitchen

End your day with a Pan-Asian feast at this relaxed **eatery** (☏020-7377 0411; www.yuukitchen. com; 29 Commercial St, E1; dishes £5-10; ⏰5.30-9.30pm Mon-Wed, noon-2.30pm & 5.30pm-late Thu-Sat, 2-4.30pm & 5.30-9pm Sun; 🍴). Don't miss the show-stopping *bao* (Taiwanese steamed buns).

For reviews see
- ◎ Sights p187
- ✖ Eating p188
- ◗ Drinking p189
- ⬚ Shopping p190

HOXTON

Crondall St
Falkirk St
Stanway St
Geffrye St
Ormsby St
Appleby St
Weymouth Tce
Dunloe St
Dunloe St
Queensbridge Rd

Hackney R

⬚ Hoxton
Cremer St

New North Rd
Pitfield St
Fanshaw St
Kingsland Rd
Diss St
Ravenscroft St

6 ✖

Ashford St
Hoxton St
Waterson St
Columbia Rd
Gosset S

Bowling Green Walk
Drysdale St
Hackney Rd
Austin St
9
Virginia Rd

Coronet
Boot St
Old St
◎ 2
SHOREDITCH
Pitfield St
Cargo
10
11 Calvert Ave
Swanfield St
Brick La

Rivington St
◀ 5
✖ 3
Charlotte Rd
Curtain Rd
Rivington St
Boundary St
Old Nichol St
Club Row
Bethnal Green Rd
7
8
Redchurch St
4

XOYO (150m)
Willow St
Tabernacle St
Leonard St
Bateman's Row
New Inn Yard

Great Eastern St
Luke St
Phipp St
Scrutton St
Sclater St
Cheshir

Paul St
Holywell Row
Scrutton St
Curtain Rd
Shoreditch High St
◎ ⬚
Shoreditch
High St

Horse & Groom
Quaker St
Buxton S

Worship St
Worship St
SPITALFIELDS
Brick La
14
⬚
Woodseer St
12 ⬚
Hanbury S

Wilson St
Clifton St
Appold St
Commercial St
Folgate St
1 ◎
Dennis Severs' House
Lamb St
Wilkes St
Princelet S

Earl St
Sun St
Exchange Sq
13 ⬚
Fournier St

Fox & Anchor (1.2km);
Fabric (1.4km)
6

Liverpool St
◎ ⬚
Bishopsgate
Artillery La
Brushfield St
Gun St

0 ———— 200 m
0 ———— 0.1 miles

Eldon St

A   B   C   D

1   2   3   4   5   6

Sights

Dennis Severs' House
HISTORIC BUILDING

1 ◉ MAP P186, B5

This extraordinary Georgian house is set up as if its occupants – a family of Huguenot silk weavers – have just walked out the door. Each of the 10 rooms is stuffed with the minutiae of everyday life from centuries past: half-drunk cups of tea, emptied but gleaming-wet oyster shells and, in perhaps unnecessary attention to detail, a used chamber pot by the bed. It's more an immersive experience than a traditional museum; explorations of the house are conducted in silence. Night-time sessions are illuminated solely by candlelight and kerosene lamps and are particularly atmospheric; book online in advance. Visits take around 45 minutes. Photography is not allowed, and there are no toilets on the premises. (☏020-7247 4013; www.dennissevershouse. co.uk; 18 Folgate St, E1; day/night £10/15; ⊘noon-2pm & 5-9pm Mon, 5-9pm Wed & Fri, noon-4pm Sun; ⓤLiverpool St)

St John's Gate
HISTORIC BUILDING

2 ◉ MAP P186, A3

This remarkable Tudor gate dates from 1504. During the 12th century, the Knights Hospitaller (a Christian and military order with a focus on providing care to the sick) established a priory here. Inside is a small museum that covers the history of the order (including rare

St John's Gate

Georgian Spitalfields

Crowded around its famous market and grand parish church, Spitalfields has long been one of the capital's most multicultural areas. Waves of Huguenot (French Protestant), Jewish, Irish and, more recently, Indian and Bangladeshi immigrants have made Spitalfields home. To get a sense of what Georgian Spitalfields was like, branch off to Princelet, Fournier, Elder and Wilkes streets. Having fled persecution in France, the Huguenots set up shop here from the late 17th century, practising their trade of silk weaving.

examples of the knights' armour), as well as its 19th-century revival in Britain as the Christian Order of St John and the foundation of St John Ambulance. (www.museum stjohn.org.uk; St John's Lane, EC1; admission free; ⏲10am-5pm, closed Sun Oct-Jun; ⓤFarringdon)

Eating

Breddos Tacos   TACOS £

3 🍴 MAP P186, A4

Started in an East London car park in 2011, Breddos found its first permanent home in Clerkenwell, dishing out some of London's best Mexican grub. Grab some friends and order each of the eight or so tacos, served in pairs, on the menu: fillings vary, but past favourites include confit pork belly, and veggie-friendly mole, queso fresco and egg. The tostadas are also exquisite. (📞020-3535 8301; www. breddostacos.com; 82 Goswell Rd, EC1; tacos from £5, mains £7.50-17; ⏲noon-3pm & 5-11pm Mon-Fri, noon-11.30pm Sat; 🖊; ⓤOld St or Farringdon)

Smoking Goat   THAI ££

4 🍴 MAP P186, C4

Trotting in on one of London's fleeting flavours of the week, Smoking Goat's modern Thai menu is top notch. The industrial-chic look of exposed brick, huge factory windows and original parquet floors surround the open kitchen. It's a tough place for the spice-shy; cool down with a cold one from the exquisite cocktail list. Don't miss the smoked five-spice chicken. (www.smokinggoatbar.com; 64 Shoreditch High St, E1; dishes £4-29; ⏲noon-3pm & 5.30-11pm, to 1am Fri & Sat, to 11pm Sun; ⓤShoreditch High St)

St John   BRITISH ££

5 🍴 MAP P186, A3

Around the corner from London's last remaining meat market, St John is the standard-bearer for nose-to-tail cuisine. With white-washed brick walls, high ceilings and simple wooden furniture, it's surely one of the most humble

Michelin-starred restaurants nywhere. The menu changes daily but is likely to include the ignature roast bone marrow and parsley salad. (☎ 020-7251 0848; www.stjohnrestaurant.com; 26 St John t, EC1; mains £17-26.50; ☷noon-3pm & 6-11pm Mon-Fri, 6-11pm Sat, 12.30-pm Sun; Ⓤ Farringdon)

Brawn

EUROPEAN ££

 MAP P186, D2

There's a French feel to this re-axed corner bistro, yet the menu wanders into Italian and Span-ish territory as well. Dishes are easonally driven and delicious, and there's an interesting selec-ion of European wine on offer. Booking ahead is recommended. ☎ 020-7729 5692; www.brawn.co; 49 Columbia Rd, E2; mains £14-22; ☷6-0.30pm Mon, noon-10.30pm Tue-Thu, noon-11pm Fri & Sat; Ⓤ Hoxton)

Beigel Bake

BAKERY £

 MAP P186, D4

This relic of the Jewish East End still does a brisk trade serving dirt-cheap homemade bagels stuffed with smoked salmon and cream cheese, salt beef and pick-es, or a handful of other fillings) to hungry shoppers and late-night poozers. There's a queue no matter the time of day or night, but the curt staff keep things moving. (☎ 071 729 0616; 159 Brick Lane, E1; filled bagels £1-5; ☷24hr; Ⓤ Shoreditch High St)

Drinking

Cocktail Trading Co   COCKTAIL BAR

8 Ⓠ MAP P186, D4

In an area famous for its edgy, don't-give-a-damn attitude, this exquisite cocktail bar stands out for its classiness and cocktail confidence. The drinks are truly unrivalled, from flavours to presentation – bottles presented in envelopes, ice cubes as big as Rubik's Cubes and so on. The decor is reminiscent of a colonial-era gentlemen's club, just warmer and more welcoming. (☎ 020-7427 6097; www.thecocktailtradingco.co.uk; 68 Bethnal Green Rd, E1; ☷5-11.30pm Mon-Wed, to midnight Thu & Fri, 2pm-midnight Sat, 2-10.30pm Sun; Ⓤ Shoreditch High St)

Drinking Directions

Shoreditch is the torch bearer of London's nightlife: there are dozens of bars, clubs and pubs, open virtually every night of the week (and until the small hours at weekends) and it can get pretty rowdy. Clerkenwell is more sedate, featuring lovely historic pubs and fine cocktail bars. Spitalfields sits somewhere in between the two extremes and tends to be defined by its City clientele on week nights and market-goers on Saturday and Sunday.

Mikkeller Bar London

CRAFT BEER

9 MAP P186, C3

Legendary Danish microbrewery Mikkeller is known for its collaborations, but its latest is next level. Mikkeller's founder met musician Rick Astley on a previous brewing project, and the two have joined forces again to open Mikkeller's first UK bar. The pub unsurprisingly opts for a Scandi-chic interior, and lyrics from Astley's songs are enshrined in golden plaques on the tables and bar. (www.mikkeller.com; 2-4 Hackney Rd, E2; ⏰noon-10.30pm Mon-Thu, to 11.30pm Fri & Sat, to 10pm Sun; Ⓤ Shoreditch High St or Old St)

Callooh Callay

COCKTAIL BAR

10 MAP P186, B3

Given it's inspired by *Jabberwocky*, Lewis Carroll's nonsensical poem, this bar's eccentric decor is to be expected, and the top-notch cocktails have placed it on the 'World's 50 Best Bars' list four times over. *Through the Looking Glass* isn't just the name of Carroll's novel here; try it yourself and see what happens. (☎020-7739 4781; www.calloohcallaybar.com; 65 Rivington St, EC2; ⏰6pm-1am; Ⓤ Old St or Shoreditch High St)

Shopping

Aida

CONCEPT STOR

11 🔒 MAP P186, B3

Brick walls, minimalist wood and metal fixtures, and pops of green from potted plants make this concept shop a delight to peruse. Indie brands abound in the form of menswear, womenswear, shoes and accessories, plus home goods, books, fragrances and skincare. Browsing's all the better with a coffee, juice or latte from the shop's cafe. (☎020-7739 2011; www. aidashoreditch.co.uk; 133 Shoreditch High St, E1; ⏰10.30am-7pm Mon-Sat, noon-6pm Sun; Ⓤ Shoreditch High St)

Libreria

BOOKS

12 🔒 MAP P186, D5

Mismatched vintage reading lamps spotlight the floor-to-ceiling canary-yellow shelves at this delightful indie bookshop, where titles are arranged according to themes like 'wanderlust', 'enchantment for the disenchanted', and 'mothers, madonnas and whores'. Cleverly placed mirrors add to the labyrinthine wonder of the space, which is punctuated with

---

Fancy a Late One?

Pubs and clubs **Fabric** (www.fabriclondon.com), **XOYO** (www.xoyo.co.uk), **Cargo** (Map p186, B3; www.cargo-london.com) and the **Horse & Groom** (Map p186, B5; www.thehorseandgroom.net) all stay open until at least 3am on weekends. For breakfast with a pint, the **Fox & Anchor** (www.foxandanchor.com) throws back its doors at 7am (8.30am on weekends).

itchens, Old Spitalfields Market

mid-century furniture that invites repose and quiet contemplation. www.libreria.io; 65 Hanbury St, E1; ⏱10am-6pm Tue & Wed, to 8pm Thu-at, 11am-6pm Sun; ⓊAldgate East)

Old Spitalfields Market

MARKET

3 🄰 MAP P186, C6

Traders have been hawking their wares here since 1638, and it's still one of London's best markets. Sundays are the biggest days, but Thursdays are good for antiques, and crates of vinyl take over every other Friday. The market upped its foodie credentials with the **Kitchens**, 10 food counters that are the perfect antidote to the mostly bland chain restaurants on the market's periphery. (www.oldspital

fieldsmarket.com; Commercial St, E1; ⏱10am-8pm Mon-Fri, to 6pm Sat, to 5pm Sun; ⓊLiverpool St, Shoreditch High St or Aldgate East)

Rough Trade East

MUSIC

14 🄰 MAP P186, D5

It's no longer directly associated with the legendary record label (home to the Smiths, the Libertines and the Strokes, among others), but this huge record shop is still tops for picking up indie, soul, electronica and alternative music. In addition to an impressive selection of CDs and vinyl, it also dispenses coffee and stages gigs and artist signings. (📞020-7392 7788; www.roughtrade.com; Old Truman Brewery, 91 Brick Lane, E1; ⏱9am-9pm Mon-Thu, to 8pm Fri, 10am-8pm Sat, 11am-7pm Sun; ⓊShoreditch High St)

Worth a Trip 🔭
Ponder the Stars at the Royal Observatory & Greenwich Park

The Royal Observatory is where the studies of the sea, stars and time converge. The prime meridian charts its line through the grounds of the observatory to divide the globe into the eastern and western hemispheres. The complex sits atop a hill within leafy and regal Greenwich Park, with iconic views of the River Thames and the skyscrapers of Canary Wharf.

☎ 020-8312 6565

www.rmg.co.uk/royal-observatory

Greenwich Park, Blackheath Ave

adult/child £16/8

⏲ 10am-5pm Sep-Jun, to 6pm Jul & Aug

Flamsteed House

Charles II ordered construction of the Christopher Wren–designed Flamsteed House, the original observatory building, on the foundations of Greenwich Castle in 1675 after closing the observatory at the Tower of London, allegedly because the ravens were pooing on the equipment. Today it contains the magnificent **Octagon Room** and the rather simple apartment where the Royal Astronomers and their families lived. On the lower levels, you'll find the **Time Galleries**, which explain how the longitude problem – how to accurately determine a ship's east–west location – was solved through astronomical means and the invention of the marine chronometer.

Meridian Courtyard

In the Meridian Courtyard, where the globe is decisively sliced into east and west, visitors can delightfully straddle both hemispheres, with one foot on either side of the meridian line. Every day, the red **Time Ball** atop the Royal Observatory drops at 1pm, as it has done since 1833.

The Greenwich meridian was selected as the global prime meridian at the International Meridian Conference in Washington, DC, in 1884. Greenwich became the world's ground zero for longitude and standard for time calculations, replacing the multiple meridians that had existed before. Greenwich was assisted in its bid by the earlier US adoption of Greenwich Mean Time for its own national time zones, though the majority of world trade already used sea charts that identified Greenwich as the prime meridian.

Camera Obscura

In a small brick structure next to the Meridian Courtyard, the camera obscura projects a live image of Queen's House (p197) – as well as the people moving around it and the boats on

★ Top Tips

o Pre-booking a combination ticket for the Royal Observatory and Cutty Sark online saves almost 25% (adult/child £23.65/11.85).

o Pack a lunch or bring goodies from Greenwich Market so you don't have to trek down the hill until you've finished the Observatory visit.

✗ Take a Break

The Astronomy Centre has a cafe, or pack a sandwich to devour in Greenwich Park. Down the hill, you can snack your way around Greenwich Market (p197).

★ Getting There

🚈 Take the DLR to Cutty Sark or Greenwich stations.

⛴ Boats run from several central London piers.

🚶 One of London's two under-river pedestrian-only tunnels links Greenwich to the Isle of Dogs.

ROYAL
OBSERVATORY
GREENWICH

SHEPHERD ● PATENTEE
53 LEADENHALL ST. LONDON

GALVANO-MAGNETIC CLOCK

The Shepherd
24-hour Gate Clock

The Time Ball

Ordnance Survey
Bench Mark

Public Standards
of Length

BRITISH YARD

TWO FEET

ONE FOOT

Prime Target

On 15 February 1894, the Royal Observatory was the unexpected target of a bomb plot. The bomber – a 26-year-old French anarchist called Martial Bourdin – managed to blow his left hand off in the bungled attack and died from his wounds soon afterwards. The choice of the Royal Observatory as a target was never understood, but it was undamaged. The bombing later found literary recognition in Joseph Conrad's novel *The Secret Agent* and the anarchist appears in the TS Eliot poem *Animula* under the name Boudin.

the Thames behind – onto a table. Enter through the thick, light-dimming curtains and close them behind you to keep the room as dark as possible.

Astronomy Centre

The southern half of the observatory contains the informative (and free) Weller Astronomy Galleries, where you can touch an object as ancient as the sun: part of the Gibeon meteorite, a mere 4.5 billion years old. Other exhibits include a 1780 orrery (mechanical model of the solar system, minus the as-yet-undiscovered Uranus and Neptune), astro documentaries and the opportunity to view the Milky Way in multiple wavelengths.

Peter Harrison Planetarium

London's only planetarium, the state-of-the-art **Peter Harrison Planetarium** (☏020-8858 4422; www.rmg.co.uk/whats-on/planetarium-shows; adult/child £10/5), can lay

out the heavens on the inside of its roof. It runs several informative shows a day, including a programme for kids, and it's best to book in advance.

Greenwich Park

Greenwich Park (www.royalparks.org.uk/parks/greenwich-park; ☉6am-sunset; ⓤGreenwich, Maze Hill or Cutty Sark) is one of London's loveliest expanses of green, with a rose garden, picturesque walking paths, a 6th-century Anglo-Saxon burial ground, and astonishing views of Canary Wharf – the financial district across the Thames – from the crown of the hill. Covering 74 hectares, it's the oldest enclosed royal park and is partly the work of André Le Nôtre, the landscape architect who designed the palace gardens of Versailles.

If you don't want to pay to enter the Meridian Courtyard, look out for the continuation of the prime meridian line, marked in metal, just outside the fence, where you can be in two hemispheres at once for free.

Walking Tour 🥾

A Wander Around Historic Greenwich

If Greenwich's grand sights belonged to a British town beyond the capital, they would elevate it to one of the top destinations in the UK. That they belong to a district of London alone naturally makes this quaint Unesco-listed area a must-see neighbourhood. Fortunately, all of Greenwich's big-hitting sights are within an easily walkable area.

Getting There

🚆 Take the DLR to Cutty Sark or Greenwich stations.

⛴ Thames Clippers boats run to Greenwich and Royal Arsenal Woolwich from several central London piers.

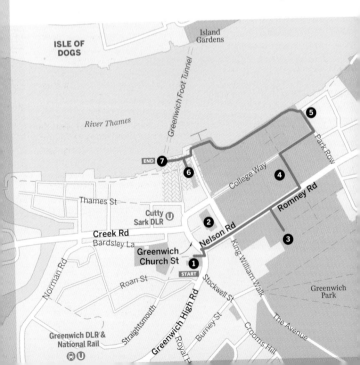

❶ St Alfege Church

Designed by Nicholas Hawksmoor to replace a 13th-century church, baroque **St Alfege** (☎ 020-8853 0687; www.st-alfege.org; Greenwich Church St; ⏰ 11am-4pm Mon-Sat, noon-4pm Sun) was consecrated in 1718 and features a restored mural by James Thornhill.

❷ Greenwich Market

Cross Greenwich Church St to **Greenwich Market** (www.greenwich market.london; College Approach; ⏰ 10am-5.30pm), one of London's smaller and more atmospheric covered markets, and snack your way through the stalls of food vendors hawking home-made Jamaican rum cake, locally sourced oysters, Ethiopian vegetarian boxes, filled Brazilian churros and so much more.

❸ National Maritime Museum & Queen's House

Walk along Nelson Rd to the **National Maritime Museum** (☎ 020-8312 6565; www.rmg.co.uk/ national-maritime-museum; Romney Rd; admission free; ⏰ 10am-5pm), which narrates the long, briny and eventful history of seafaring Brit-ain. Continue the seafaring theme with a stop at nearby **Queen's House** (www.rmg.co.uk/queens-house; Romney Rd; admission free; ⏰ 10am-5pm), which has a gallery of portraits and other pieces with a maritime bent.

❹ Painted Hall

Cross Romney Rd to the grounds of the Old Royal Naval College, Greenwich's grandest collection of buildings. The recently restored **Painted Hall** (☎ 020-8269 4799; www.ornc.org; adult/child £12/free; ⏰ 10am-5pm), completed in 1726, is an over-the-top banqueting space covered floor to ceiling with the largest painting in Europe.

❺ Trafalgar Tavern

Head to the Thames walkway and east to the elegant **Trafalgar Tavern** (☎ 020-3887 9886; www.tra falgartavern.co.uk; Park Row; ⏰ noon-11pm Mon-Thu, to 1am Fri, 9am-1am Sat, to 11pm Sun), with crystal chandeliers, nautical decor and windows overlooking the Thames.

❻ Cutty Sark

Follow the scenic path between the Thames and the Old Royal Naval College grounds to the **Cutty Sark** (☎ 020-8312 6565; www.rmg.co.uk/ cuttysark; King William Walk; adult/child £15/7.50; ⏰ 10am-5pm), the last of the great clipper ships to sail between China and England in the 19th century.

❼ Greenwich Foot Tunnel

Descend to the **Greenwich Foot Tunnel** (Cutty Sark Gardens; ⏰ 24hr) and cross under the river to the Isle of Dogs for stupefying views of Greenwich from the north shore.

Worth a Trip 🔭

Tour Regal Hampton Court Palace

London's most spectacular Tudor palace, 16th-century Hampton Court Palace is steeped in history, from the grand living quarters of Henry VIII to the spectacular gardens, complete with a 300-year-old maze. One of the best days out London has to offer, the palace is mandatory for anyone with an interest in British history, Tudor architecture or gorgeous landscaped gardens. Set aside plenty of time to do it justice.

www.hrp.org.uk/hampton courtpalace

Hampton Court Palace, KT8

adult/child £24/12

🕙10am-6pm Apr-Oct, to 4.30pm Nov-Mar

Entering the Palace

Passing through the magnificent main gate, you arrive first in the **Base Court** and beyond that the **Clock Court**, named after its 16th-century astronomical clock. The panelled rooms and arched doorways in the **Young Henry VIII's Story** upstairs from Base Court provide a rewarding introduction: note the Tudor graffiti on the fireplace. Off Base Court to the right as you enter, and acquired by Charles I in 1629, Andrea Magenta's nine-painting series **The Triumphs of Caesar** portray Julius Caesar returning to Rome in a triumphant procession.

Henry VIII's State Apartments

The stairs inside Anne Boleyn's Gateway lead up to Henry VIII's Apartments, including the stunning **Great Hall**. The **Horn Room**, hung with impressive antlers, leads to the **Great Watching Chamber** where guards controlled access to the king.

Royal Pew & Henry VIII's Crown

Henry VIII's dazzling gemstone-encrusted crown has been re-created – the original was melted down by Oliver Cromwell – and sits in the Royal Pew (open 10am to 5.30pm Monday to Saturday and 12.30pm to 3pm Sunday), which overlooks the beautiful **Chapel Royal** (still a place of worship after 450 years).

Tudor Kitchens & Great Wine Cellar

Also dating from Henry's day are the delightful Tudor kitchens, once used to rustle up meals for a royal household of some 1200 people. Don't miss the Great Wine Cellar, which handled the 300 barrels each of ale and wine consumed here annually in the mid-16th century.

★ **Top Tips**

o Check the website for activities and join a tour with a costumed guide.

o Bushy Park (www.royalparks.org.uk), a 445-hectare semi-wild expanse with herds of deer is right next door.

✕ **Take a Break**

There are three cafes within the palace grounds: the **Tiltyard Cafe**, the **Privy Kitchen** and the **Fountain Court Cafe**. The gardens are huge, so pack a picnic if it's sunny.

★ **Getting There**

🚃 Hampton Court train station has services to/from London Waterloo.

⛴ Thames River Boats (www.wpsa.co.uk) runs services here from Westminster (adult/child £19/9.50, three to four hours, April to September).

Events & Activities

Check the schedule for details on spectacular shows and events, including Tudor jousting, falconry displays, ghost tours, garden adventures and family trails. In summer, fun 15- to 20-minute shire-horse-drawn **charabanc tours** (adult/child £6/3) depart from the East Front Garden between 11am and 5pm. Luna Cinema (www.thelunacinema.com) hosts outdoor films in summer at the palace. From November to mid-January you can glide (or slide) around the palace's glittering ice rink.

Cumberland Art Gallery

The restored Cumberland Suite off Clock Court is the venue for a staggering display of artworks from the Royal Collection, including Rembrandt's *Self-Portrait in a Flat Cap* (1642) and Sir Anthony van Dyck's *Charles I on Horseback* (c 1635–36).

William III's & Mary II's Apartments

A tour of William III's Apartments, completed by Wren in 1702, takes you up the grand **King's Staircase**. Highlights include the **King's Presence Chamber**, dominated by a throne backed with scarlet hangings. The sumptuous **King's Great Bedchamber**, with a bed topped with ostrich plumes, and the King's Closet (where His Majesty's toilet has a velvet seat) should not be missed. The unique **Chocolate Kitchens** were built for William and Mary in about 1689. William's wife Mary II had her own apartments, accessible via the fabulous **Queen's Staircase** (decorated by William Kent).

Georgian Private Apartments

The Georgian Rooms were used by George II and Queen Caroline on the court's last visit to the palace in 1737. Do not miss the superb Tudor **Wolsey Closet** with its early 16th-century ceiling and painted panels, commissioned by Henry VIII.

Cartoon Gallery

The Cartoon Gallery used to display the original Raphael Cartoons (now in the V&A); nowadays it's just the late-17th-century copies.

Gardens & Maze

Beyond the palace are the stunning gardens; keep an eye out for the **Real Tennis Court**, dating from the 1620s. Originally created for William and Mary, the **Kitchen Garden** is a magnificent re-creation.

No one should leave Hampton Court without losing themselves in the 800m-long **maze** (adult/child £4.50/3; ⊙10am-4.15pm Apr-Oct, to 3.45pm Nov-Mar), also accessible to those not entering the palace.

Great Hall

Survival Guide

Before You Go

Book Your Stay

o Shoreditch, Kensington and South Bank are great places to stay.

o London has some fantastic hotels, but demand often outstrips supply: book ahead, especially during summer and holidays.

o Budgets under £100 per night get you a hostel bed (some are contemporary and stylish) or basic B&B. Look for online deals, especially for quieter nights (eg Sundays).

o B&Bs can have boutique-style charm, a lovely old building setting and a personal level of service.

o For stays of a week or more, serviced apartments and short-term lets can be economical.

Useful Websites

o **Visit London** (www. visitlondon.com) Huge range of listings; official tourism portal.

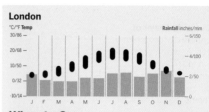

London

°C/°F Temp — Rainfall inches/mm

When to Go

o **Winter (Dec–Feb)**
Cold, short days with rain and occasional snow. Museums and attractions quieter.

o **Spring (Mar–May)**
Milder weather; trees in blossom, gardens in bloom. Major sights begin to get busy.

o **Summer (Jun–Aug)**
Warm, sunny and light until late. High season. Expect crowds, but London's parks are lovely.

o **Autumn (Sep–Nov)**
Mild, sunny and colourful. Kids go back to school.

o **London Town** (www. londontown.com) Last-minute offers on boutique hotels and B&Bs.

o **London Bed & Breakfast** (www.londonbb. com) B&B in private homes across the city.

o **Lonely Planet** (lonelyplanet.com/england/london/hotels) Hotel recommendations.

Best Budget

Qbic (www.qbichotels. com/london-city) Well-designed little rooms available at a steal if

booked early enough.

Clink78 (www.clink hostels.com/london/clink78) Heritage hostel in a former magistrates court.

Generator London (www.staygenerator. com/hostels/london) Large poshtel near Bloomsbury.

Safestay Holland Park (www.safestay.com/london-kensington-holland-park) A bright addition to the only surviving wing of a Jacobean mansion.

Best Midrange

CitizenM Tower of London (www.citizenm. com/destinations/ london/tower-of-london-hotel) Small but perfectly formed rooms, some with killer views.

Hoxton Hotel Southwark (www.thehoxton. com/london/south-wark/hotels) Outstanding value, great location and gorgeous fit-out.

40 Winks (www.40winks.org) Whimsically decorated boutique B&B in the East End.

Petersham (www. petershamhotel.co.uk) Bucolic Richmond is the perfect spot to unwind.

Best Top End

The Ned (www.thened. com) Heritage in the central financial district.

Number Sixteen (www.firmdalehotels. com/hotels/london/ number-sixteen) Sophisticated and colourful with an idyllic garden.

Hazlitt's (www.hazlitts hotel.com) Old-world elegance in a terrific location.

Beaumont (www. thebeaumont.com) Art Deco opulence and an excellent cocktail bar.

Ritz London (www. theritzlondon.com) Spectacular location by Green Park with rooms filled with antiques.

Arriving in London

Heathrow Airport

Some 15 miles west of central London, Heathrow Airport (LHR; www.heathrow airport.com) is one of the world's busiest, with four passenger terminals (numbered 2 to 5). It's Britain's main airport for international flights.

Underground Three Underground stations on the Piccadilly line serve Heathrow: one for Terminals 2 and 3, another for Terminal 4, and the terminus for Terminal 5. The cheapest way of getting to Heathrow; one-way paper tickets cost £6, Oyster or Contactless peak/off-peak costs £5.10/3.10. The journey

to central London takes 45 minutes and trains depart every three to nine minutes. From the airport, it runs from just after 5am to just after midnight (11.28pm Sunday), to the airport it runs from 5.09am to 11.54pm (11pm on Sunday); Piccadilly line trains run all night Friday and Saturday, with reduced frequency.

Train The Heathrow Express (one way/return £25/37; children free) links Heathrow with Paddington train station every 15 minutes. Trains run from around 5am to between 11pm and midnight.

Bus National Express (www.nationalexpress. com) coaches (one-way from £6, 40 to 90 minutes, every 30 to 60 minutes) link Heathrow Central bus station with London Victoria coach station. The first bus leaves Heathrow Central bus station (at Terminals 2 and 3) at 4.20am, with the last departure just after 10pm. The first bus leaves Victoria at 3am, the last at around 12.30am. At night, the N9 bus (£1.50, 1¼ hours, every 20 minutes) connects Heathrow Central bus station (and Heathrow Terminal 5) with central London, terminating at Aldwych.

Taxi A metered black-cab trip to/from central London will cost between £50 and £100 and take 45 minutes to an hour, depending on traffic.

Gatwick Airport

Located some 30 miles south of central London, Gatwick (LGW; www.gatwick airport.com) is smaller than Heathrow and is Britain's number-two airport, mainly for international flights. The North and South Terminals are linked by a 24-hour shuttle train (three minutes).

Train National Rail (www.nationalrail. co.uk) has regular train services to/from London Bridge (30 minutes, every 15 to 30 minutes), London King's Cross (55 minutes, every 15 to 30 minutes) and London Victoria (30 minutes, every 10 to 15 minutes). Fares vary depending on the time of travel and

the train company, but allow £10 to £20 for a single.

○ Gatwick Express trains (£19.50 one-way without advanced booking) run every 15 minutes from the station near Gatwick South Terminal to London Victoria. From the airport, there are services between 5.45am and 12.20am. From Victoria, they leave between 5am and 11.30am. The journey takes 30 minutes.

Bus National Express (www.nationalexpress. com) coaches run throughout the day from Gatwick to London Victoria coach station (one way from £8). Services depart hourly around the clock. Journey time is between 80 minutes and two hours, depending on traffic.

Taxi A metered black-cab to/from central London costs around £100 and takes just over an hour. Uber and minicab companies are usually cheaper.

Stansted Airport

Stansted (STN; www. stanstedairport.com) is 35 miles northeast

of central London in the direction of Cambridge. An international airport, Stansted serves a multitude of mainly European destinations and is served primarily by low-cost carriers such as Ryanair.

Train Stansted Express (www.stanstedexpress. com) service (45 minutes, every 15 to 30 minutes, £19.40) links the airport and Liverpool St station. From the airport, trains leave from 5.30am to 12.30am. Trains depart Liverpool St station from 3.40am to 11.25pm.

Bus National Express (www.nationalexpress. com) coaches run around the clock, offering well over 100 services per day.

○ Airbus A6 runs to Westminster (£10, around 60 to 90 minutes, every 20 minutes) via Marble Arch, Paddington, Baker St and Golders Green.

○ Airbus A7 runs to Victoria coach station (£10, around 60 to 90 minutes, every 20 minutes), via Waterloo and Southwark.

o Airbus A8 runs to Liverpool St station (one way from £7, 60 to 80 minutes, every 30 minutes), via Bethnal Green, Shoreditch High St and Mile End. Airbus A9 goes to Stratford (£7, 50 minutes).

o Airport Bus Express (from £8, 80 minutes) runs every 30 minutes to London Victoria coach station, Liverpool Street and Stratford.

o EasyBus (www. easybus.co.uk) runs services to Baker St and Old St Tube stations (£2, 90 minutes, every 15 minutes).

o Terravision (www. terravision.eu) links Stansted to Liverpool St train station (from £9, 55 minutes), King's Cross (from £7, 75 minutes) and Victoria coach station (from £10, two hours) every 20 to 40 minutes between 6am and 1am. Wi-fi is available on all buses.

Taxi A metered black cab trip to/from central London costs around £130 and takes at least an hour, depending on traffic and your destination. Uber and other minicabs are cheaper.

St Pancras International Station

Eurostar (www.euro star.com) high-speed passenger rail service linking London St Pancras International with Paris, Brussels, Amsterdam and other European cities. It has up to 19 daily departures. Fares vary greatly, from £29 one way standard class to around £245 one way for a fully flexible business premier ticket (prices based on return journeys). Join Eurostar Snap for deals if you have some flexibility around dates and times of travel.

Getting Around

Underground, DLR & Overground

o Public transport in London is excellent, if pricey.

o The London Underground ('the Tube'; 11 colour-coded lines) is part of a system that also includes Docklands Light Railway (DLR; www.tfl.gov.uk/dlr; a driverless overhead train operating in the eastern part of the city) and the Overground network (mostly outside of Zone 1 and sometimes underground).

o It is overall the quickest and easiest way of getting around the city. It's always cheaper to travel with an Oyster Card or contactless payments (unless you're paying international transaction fees) than buying a paper ticket. Children under 11 travel free.

o First trains operate from around 5.30am Monday to Saturday and 6.45am Sunday. Last trains leave around 12.30am Monday to Saturday and 11.30pm Sunday.

o Selected lines (the Victoria and Jubilee lines, plus most of the Piccadilly, Central and Northern lines) run all night on Friday and Saturday on what is called the 'Night Tube'.

o London is divided into nine concentric fare zones.

Bus

o Red double-decker buses afford great views of the city, but the going can be slow in heavy traffic.

o There are excellent bus maps at bus stops detailing routes and destinations serving the local area.

o The City Mapper app is also very helpful for trip planning and live updates on bus arrival times.

o Cash cannot be used on London's buses. Instead you must pay with an Oyster Card, Travelcard or a contactless payment card. Bus fares are a flat £1.50, no matter the distance travelled.

o Bus services normally operate from 5am to 11.30pm.

o More than 50 night-bus routes (prefixed with the letter 'N') run from around 11.30pm to 5am.

o Oxford Circus, Tottenham Court Rd and Trafalgar Sq are the main hubs for night routes.

o Children under 11 travel free; 11- to 15-year-olds are half-price if registered on an accompanying adult's Oyster Card (register at a Zone 1 train station or at Heathrow Tube stations).

Bicycle

o Santander Cycles (www.tfl.gov.uk/modes/cycling/santander-cycles) are straightforward and particularly useful for visitors.

o Pick up a bike from one of the 750 docking stations dotted around the capital. Drop it off at another docking station.

o The access fee is £2 for 24 hours. Insert your debit or credit card in the docking station to pay your access fee.

o The first 30 minutes are free, then it's £2 for any additional period of 30 minutes (the pricing structure encourages short journeys).

o Take as many bikes as you like during your access period (24 hours), leaving five minutes between each trip.

o If the docking station is full, consult the terminal to find available docking points nearby.

o Uber also offers short-term bike hire called JUMP (www.jump.com/gb/en).

Taxi

o Black cabs are available for hire when the yellow sign above the windscreen is lit; just stick your arm out to signal one.

o Fares are metered, with the flag-fall charge of £3.20 (covering the first 248m during a weekday), rising by increments of 20p for each subsequent 124m.

o Fares are more expensive in the evenings and overnight.

o You can tip taxi drivers 10% of the fare, but most Londoners simply round up to the nearest pound.

o Apps such as Gett (www.gett.com/uk/city/london) use your smartphone's GPS to locate the nearest black cab.

o ComCab (www.comcab-london.co.uk) operates one of the largest fleets of black cabs in town.

o Rideshares and minicabs, which are also licensed, are cheaper competitors to black cabs, but cannot be hailed on the street. They must be hired by phone, online or via an app.

Oyster Card

The Oyster Card is a smart card on which you can store credit towards 'prepay' fares, as well as Travelcards valid for periods from a day to a year. Oyster Cards are valid across the entire public transport network in London.

All you need to do when entering a station is touch your card on a reader (which has a yellow circle with the image of an Oyster Card on it) and then touch again on your way out. The system will then deduct the appropriate amount of credit from your card, as necessary. For bus journeys, you only need to touch once upon boarding. Note that some train stations don't have exit turnstiles, so you will need to tap out on the reader before leaving the station; if you forget, you will be hugely overcharged.

The benefit lies in the fact that fares for Oyster Card users are lower than standard ones. If you are making many journeys during the day, you will never pay more than the appropriate Travelcard (peak or off-peak) once the daily 'price cap' has been reached.

o Oyster Cards can be bought (£5 refundable deposit required) and topped up at any Underground station, travel information centre or shop displaying the Oyster logo. To get your deposit back along with any remaining credit, simply return your Oyster Card at a ticket booth.

o Contactless bank cards and Apple/Google Pay can now be used directly on Oyster Card readers and are subject to the same Oyster fares. The advantage is that you don't have to bother with buying, topping up and then returning an Oyster Card, but foreign visitors should bear in mind the cost of international transactions.

o Minicabs don't have meters; there's usually a fare set by the dispatcher. Make sure you ask before setting off.

o Apps such as Kabbee allow you to pre-book a minicab.

Boat

Thames Clippers

(www.thamesclippers. com) boats run regular services between Embankment, Waterloo (London Eye), Blackfriars, Bankside (Shakespeare's Globe), London Bridge, Tower Bridge, Canary Wharf, Greenwich, North Greenwich and Woolwich piers (all zones adult/child £8.70/4.35), from 6.55am to around midnight (from 9.29am weekends). Check out the 'Roamer' ticket if you're doing more than one trip.

Westminster Passenger Services Association (www.wpsa.co.uk) boats run between April and September to Hampton Court Palace from Westminster Pier in central London (via Kew and Richmond).

Car & Motorcycle

o Expensive parking charges, traffic jams, high petrol prices, efficient traffic wardens and wheel-clampers make driving unattractive for most Londoners.

o There is a congestion charge of £11.50 per day in central London. For full details check www.tfl.gov.uk/roadusers/congestioncharging.

o It is illegal to use a mobile phone to call or text while driving (using a hands-free device to talk on your mobile is permitted).

o Cars drive on the left in the UK.

o All drivers and passengers must wear seat belts and motorcyclists must wear a helmet.

Essential Information

Accessible Travel

o For travellers with access needs, London is a frustrating mix of user-friendliness and head-in-the-sand disinterest. Visitors with vision, hearing or cognitive impairments will find their needs met in a piecemeal fashion.

o New hotels and modern tourist attractions are legally required to be accessible to people in wheelchairs, but many historic buildings, B&Bs and guesthouses are in older buildings, which are hard or prohibitively expensive to adapt.

o As a result of hosting the 2012 Olympics and Paralympics, and thanks to a forward-looking tourist board in VisitEngland, things are improving all the time.

o Around a quarter of Tube stations, half of overground stations, most piers, all tram stops, the Emirates Air Line (cable car) and all DLR stations have step-free access.

o Buses can be lowered to street level when they stop and wheelchair users travel free.

o All black cabs are wheelchair-accessible, but power wheelchair users should note that the space is tight and sometimes headroom is insufficient.

o Guide dogs are universally welcome on public transport and in hotels, cafes, restaurants, sights, attractions etc.

o For more information, download Lonely Planet's free Accessible Travel guide from: shop.lonelyplanet.com/products/accessible-travel-online-resources.

Business Hours

Banks 9am–5pm Monday to Friday

Post offices 9am–5.30pm Monday to Friday and 9am–noon Saturday

Pubs & bars 11am–11pm (many are open later)

Restaurants noon–2.30pm and 6–11pm

Sights 10am–6pm

Shops 9am–7pm Monday tp Saturday, noon–6pm Sunday

Discount Cards

London Pass (www.londonpass.com; 1/2/3/6/10 days £75/99/125/169/199) offers free entry and queue jumping at major attractions; check the website for details.

o Passes can be tailored to include use of the Underground and buses.

Electricity

Type G
230V/50Hz

Emergencies

Dial ☎999 to call the police, fire brigade or ambulance.

Money

o Most purchases are made via electronic payments, but a few places will have a sign saying 'cash only'.

o The unit of currency in the UK is the pound sterling (£). One pound sterling consists of 100 pence (known as 'p').

o Notes come in denominations of £5, £10, £20 and £50; coins are 1p, 2p, 5p, 10p, 20p, 50p, £1 and £2.

ATMs

o Generally accept Visa, MasterCard, Cirrus or Maestro cards. There is usually a transaction surcharge for cash withdrawals with foreign cards.

o Non-bank-run ATMs that charge £1.50 to £2 per transaction are usually found inside shops (and are particularly expensive for foreign bank cards). Look for 'Free cash' signs to avoid these.

Changing Money

o Best places are local post-office branches, where no commission is charged.

o You can also change money in most high-street banks and some travel agencies, as well as at the numerous bureaux de change throughout the city.

Credit & Debit Cards

o Credit and debit cards are accepted almost universally, from restaurants and bars to shops and taxis.

o American Express and Diners Club are far less

widely used than Visa and MasterCard.

o Contactless cards and smartphone payments are increasingly widespread (look for the wi-fi–like symbol on cards, shops, taxis, buses, the Underground, rail services and other transport options). Transactions are limited to a maximum of £30.

Tipping

o Many restaurants add a 'discretionary' service charge to your bill.

o In places that don't automatically add this, you are expected to leave a 10% tip (unless service was unsatisfactory).

o There's no expectation to tip at the pub for drinks service.

Public Holidays

Most attractions and businesses close for a couple of days over Christmas and sometimes Easter. Some places close on bank-holiday Mondays.

New Year's Day
1 January

Good Friday
Late March/April

Dos & Don'ts

Although largely informal in their everyday dealings, Londoners do observe some (unspoken) rules of etiquette.

Strangers Unless asking for directions, British people generally won't start a conversation at bus stops or on Tube platforms. More latitude is given to non-British people.

Queues The British don't tolerate queue jumping. Any attempt to do so will receive tutting and protest.

Tube Stand on the right and pass on the left while riding an Underground escalator.

Bargaining Haggling over the price of goods (but not food) is OK in markets, but non-existent in shops.

Punctuality It's not good form to turn up more than 10 minutes late for drinks or dinner. If you're unavoidably late, keep everyone in the loop.

Apologise The British love apologising. If you bump into someone on the tube, say sorry; they may apologise back, even if it's your fault.

Easter Monday
Late March/April

May Day Holiday
First Monday in May

Spring Bank Holiday
Last Monday in May

Summer Bank Holiday
Last Monday in August

Christmas Day
25 December

Boxing Day
26 December

Safe Travel

London's fairly safe, so exercising common sense should be enough to avoid any incidents.

Carry hand sanitiser and a face mask, as many establishments expect you to wear one.

Pre-booking tickets and restaurant sittings also covers you for Covid-19 track-and-trace.

Smoking

○ Smoking is forbidden in all enclosed public places.

○ Pubs sometimes have a designated smoking spot outside, often on the pavement.

○ A lot of venues also have no-vaping policies. Vaping is not allowed on public transport either.

Telephone

○ The rare public phone, should you need one, accepts coins or credit cards.

○ British Telecom's famous red phone boxes survive in conservation areas only (notably Westminster).

Calling London

○ London's area code is ☏020, followed by an eight-digit number beginning with 7 (central London), 8 (Greater London) or 3 (nongeographic). You only need to dial the ☏020 when you are calling London from elsewhere in the UK or if you're dialling from a mobile.

○ To call London from abroad, dial your country's international access code, +44 (the UK's country code), +20 (dropping the initial 0 from the area code), followed by the eight-digit landline number.

Mobile Phones

It's usually better to buy a local SIM card from any mobile-phone shop, though in order to do that your handset from home must be compatible and unlocked.

Tourist Information

Visit London (www.visitlondon.com) can fill you in on everything from attractions and events to tours and accommodation. Kiosks dotted about the city can also provide maps and brochures; some branches are able to book theatre tickets.

Heathrow Airport Tourist Information Centre (www.visitlondon.com/tag/tourist-information-centre; Terminal 1, 2 & 3 Underground station concourse; 7.30am-8.30pm) Information on transport, tours, accommodation and more. You can also buy Oyster cards, Travelcards and bus passes here.

o King's Cross St Pancras Station, Liverpool Street Station, Victoria Station and Heathrow also have Tourist Information Centres.

Visas

o Immigration to the UK is becoming tougher, particularly for those seeking to work or study. Check www.gov.uk/check-uk-visa, or your local British embassy, for the most up-to-date information.

Responsible Travel

Overtourism

o Travel outside the summer peak to avoid crowds and bag a bargain on accommodation.

o Pre-book any must-see attractions, even the free ones.

o Whenever you can, walk rather than crush into a bus or Tube.

o Explore more: almost every borough boasts incredible historic sites, beautiful parks and gardens, and world-class dining opportunities.

Support Local

o Buy from Black owned businesses in London (www.blackownedlondon.com/map).

o Support a Big Issue (www.bigissue.com) vendor with a £3 magazine purchase.

o Most high streets have charity shops selling vintage items that help raise money for different causes.

o Download the award-winning app Never-spoons (https://neverspoons.app) to find independently owned pubs and bars.

o Check out Time Out's 'Love Local' campaign: championing small independent businesses that make London what it is.

Leave a Light Footprint

o Bring your own fabric facemask: you'll need it to enter many attractions.

o Look out for water refill fountains – often at major train stations.

o Download the Santander Cycles app and hire one of 12,000 bikes from 800 docking stations in London.

Behind the Scenes

Send Us Your Feedback

We love to hear from travellers – your comments help make our books better. We read every word, and we guarantee that your feedback goes straight to the authors. Visit **lonelyplanet.com/contact** to submit your updates and suggestions.

Note: We may edit, reproduce and incorporate your comments in Lonely Planet products such as guidebooks, websites and digital products, so let us know if you don't want your comments reproduced or your name acknowledged. For a copy of our privacy policy visit lonelyplanet.com/privacy.

Steve's Thanks

Many thanks to my fellow London writers, in particular Damian Harper. Kevin Bond read the Music Scene chapter and made valuable suggestions. Fellow Blue Badge Tourist Guides who vetted the Understand chapters for mistakes and/or omissions include David Thompson, Diane Burstein Lynch, Sarah Ciacci and Pepe Martinez. I am very grateful for their assistance. As always, I'd like to state my admiration, gratitude and great love for my now husband Michael Rothschild, as much a Londoner as I.

Damian's Thanks

Many thanks to everyone who helped and offered tips, including my co-authors, the ever-helpful staff at the Natural History Museum, Amaya Wang, Polly Bussell, Freya Barry, Tania Patel, Norman MacDonald, Penny Aikens, Bill

This Book

This 7th edition of Lonely Planet's *Pocket London* guidebook was researched and written by Steve Fallon, Damian Harper, Lauren Keith, MaSovaida Morgan and Tasmin Waby. The previous two editions were also written by Steve and Damian, along with Peter Dragicevich and Emilie Filou. This guidebook was produced by the following:

Senior Product Editor Sandie Kestell

Regional Senior Cartographer Mark Griffiths

Cartographers Dave Conolly, Julie Sheridan

Product Editors Saralinda Turner, Bruce Evans

Book Designers Fergal

Condon, Hannah Blackie

Assisting Editors Judith Bamber, Amy Lynch, Brana Vladisavljevic, Simon Williamson

Cover Researcher Brendan Dempsey-Spencer

Thanks to Barbara Delissen, Karen Henderson, John Ingleby, Doug Rimington, Sonia Kapoor, Angela Tinson

...Moran, Hollie and the excellent staff at Japan House, Shannon and James Peake. And big thanks to Tim Harper for his fine suggestions, and Emma Harper too.

Lauren's Thanks

Cheers to Megan for the pints, pep talks and expert 'souf' London advice; to GG for always being up for one more sharing plate; to Tasmin and MaSovaida for eternal immoral support and heading into the future wearing red lippy; to Thomas for being a Sunday-night rooftop bar yes-man; to Sandie for allowing me to explore more; and to my own silly heart for leading me to this beautiful city 10 years ago in the first place.

MaSovaida's Thanks

Deepest thanks to the wonderful souls who made this dream assignment the delight that it was. Love and gratitude are due in particular to James Thorpe, Osi and Mat; Anna Castelaz, Travis Levius, Shirin Beheshti; Nazanin Shahnavaz, Austin Milne, Rosaline Shahnavaz, Maman Simin & Baba Reza; Ali Lemer, Jo and Al; Megan Eaves, Dan, Angus; Mike, Debbie and B; Max and Ro; and Russ. Big hugs and love to my fellow former SheDEs, Tasmin and Lauren, for the immoral support and insightful feedback through frenzied WhatsApp chats. Finally, heartfelt thanks to Sandie for allowing me to return, once again, to my heart's home.

Tasmin's Thanks

First thanks to Sandie for this amazing opportunity, and the amazing Lonely Planet team for making it happen. Big thanks to my co-writers for their advice, insights and feedback, especially Lauren who kept me sane and MaSovaida who kept me company. Thanks to everyone who's ever helped me out in London, making sense (and softening the edges) of this chaotic, historic capital: you know who you are (that includes you Dane). Cheers to my two fabulous little ladies, Willa and Maisie (and their brave mate, Rosa), who accompanied me on some of my research trips to identify the best places to eat, shop, rest and play. And finally to Hugh: thank you for, well, everything.

Acknowledgements

Cover photograph: The Shard (designed by Renzo Piano), Christian Kober/AWL Images ©

Photographs pp38-9 (from left): Joe Kuis/Shutterstock ©; Alexey Fedorenko/Shutterstock ©; cowardlion/Shutterstock ©; TK Kurikawa/Shutterstock ©

Index

See also separate subindexes for:

⊗ **Eating p219**

◉ **Drinking p219**

✪ **Entertainment p220**

🔒 **Shopping p220**

Index

Lauren Keith

St Paul's & City of London; Tate Modern & South Bank Lauren is a writer and journalist who called London home for nearly a decade before selling everything she owned in 2019 to travel around the world as a digital nomad. Before hitting the road, she previously worked in Lonely Planet's London office as the Destination Editor for the Middle East and North Africa.

MaSovaida Morgan

Shoreditch & the East End MaSovaida is a travel journalist whose wayfaring tendencies have taken her to more than 55 countries across all seven continents. As a Lonely Planet author, she contributes to guidebooks on destinations throughout Southeast Asia, the Middle East, Europe and the Americas. Previously, she worked as an editor for newspapers and NGOs, and was awarded a Fulbright Fellowship in 2012 to study publishing and digital media at University of the Arts London, where she earned a master's degree. Follow her on Instagram @MaSovaida.

Tasmin Waby

Westminster Abbey & Westminster; National Gallery & Covent Garden; British Museum & Bloomsbury Born in London to Kiwi parents, Tasmin somehow ended up becoming an Australian. She now splits her time between London and Melbourne. As well as writing about her passions – food, sustainability, travel and culture – Tasmin loves travelling to new places; sometimes alone and sometimes with her kids in tow. When not on assignment, she lives on a narrowboat and is raising two ridiculously fun children and a fat Russian Blue cat called Millie. Tasmin also wrote the Survival Guide section.

Our Writers

Steve Fallon

Regent's Park & Camden After two decades of living in the centre of the known universe – East London – Steve cockney-rhymes in his sleep, eats jellied eel for brekkie, drinks lager by the bucketful and dances round the occasional handbag. As always, he did everything the hard/fun way: walking the walks, seeing the sights, sniffing through hotels, digesting lots and taking (some) advice from friends, colleagues and the occasional taxi driver. Steve is also a London-qualified Blue Badge Tourist Guide (www.steveslondon.com).

Damian Harper

Kensington Museums Damian has been writing for Lonely Planet for over two decades, contributing to titles as diverse as *China, Ireland, Mallorca, Hong Kong* and *Great Britain*. A seasoned guidebook writer, Damian has penned articles for numerous newspapers and magazines, including the *Guardian* and the *Daily Telegraph,* and currently makes Surrey, England, his home. A self-taught trumpet novice, his other hobbies include collecting modern first editions, photography and Taekwondo. Follow Damian on Instagram (damian. harper). Damian also wrote the Plan Your Trip section.

Published by Lonely Planet Global Limited
CRN 554153
7th edition – Feb 2022
ISBN 978 1 787017 40 5
© Lonely Planet 2022 Photographs © as indicated 2022
10 9 8 7 6 5 4 3 2 1
Printed in Malaysia

Although the authors and Lonely Planet have taken all reasonable care in preparing this book, we make no warranty about the accuracy or completeness of its content and, to the maximum extent permitted, disclaim all liability arising from its use.